A Complete Guide To A Successful Life-Style Change
Health, Wealth, Love And Happiness

by Dr. Ingrid D. Hicks

African American Images
Chicago, Illinois

Cover Illustration by Harold Carr

Photo Credits: William Hall

First Edition First Printing

Text Copyright 1991 by Ingrid D. Hicks

$9.95 now 7-7-92 (dh)

DEDICATION

To my mother
Barbara Hicks,
and African American women
everywhere
who make all this
possible.

Acknowledgments

To the staff of African American Images, in particular Dr. Jawanza Kunjufu who believed in this project enough to publish it.

To all of my wonderfully supportive friends, particularly Selena Elzy, Katy Gorham, Lula Robinson, and Quincy Tharps who are always there for me.

I especially want to thank Fannie LeFlore and Joyce Evans for my first media exposure. A special thanks to Kathy Tracy, my assistant and secretary, who put up with "chicken scratch writing," "garbled dictation," and "sudden deadlines."

TABLE OF CONTENTS

INTRODUCTION

Black women: beautiful, powerful, black women. At last, a book has been written that speaks to African American women's issues surrounding relationships and work. Given our unique status, we are now special enough to learn effective problem solving and generate choices in our lives. *For Black Women Only...* is targeted for every Black woman: single, partnered, divorced, widowed, or parented. The unemployed, the underemployed, the employed, and the entrepreneur are represented as well. The book is important because most self-help books are targeted toward white women; if you stroll through any bookstore's self-help section, most of what you'll find will be books written by and for White women. This book examines our issues because it was written by and for us!

For Black Women Only... is broken into three sections: our relationships (Mothers, fathers, siblings, friends, lovers, kids--all of them!); our work (from AFDC to CEO); and the ABC's of Empowerment (we need to relearn our ABC's and 1-2-3's!!!). For Black Women Only...is informational but also a fun read. The book includes quotes from famous Black women such as Oprah Winfrey, Maya Angelou, Wyomia Tyus, Jewell Jackson-McCabe and Lena Horne. It highlights famous African American artists, writers, athletes, actresses, and singers as well as political and social figures. One of the wonderful things about African-American women is that we excel as a group in so many different areas. We have been the backbone of traditional groups such as the NAACP, Urban League, sororities such as Delta Sigma Theta and Alpha Kappa Alpha. Our heritage has been preserved in academic institutions such as Spelman College and Howard University, and documented in libraries such as the New York City Library's Schomberg collection, and shown in places like the DuSable Museum in Chicago. We are achievers. The book contains references to all of that; but more importantly, it contains many, many letters from you--African American women nationwide--describing your experiences in your professional lives and loves.

Moreover, each chapter (I like to think of it as a lesson) ends with three basic steps to changing your relationships and work situations.

Relationships vs. Work

Our relationships represent the most private and public parts of us. So much is based on how we perceive ourselves, but more often, how others perceive us. It is positive thinking to believe that if you believe in yourself, others will believe in you--you should, but it is more complicated than that. People see us as Black before anything else and as a result that is usually in a negative fashion. We, indeed, have to "overcome our Blackness." For example, in comparing our relationships and work situations, White women are usually seen as aggressive at home and more passive in the workplace. (Remember it is only recently they were in the workplace.) Conversely, African American women in general are seen as aggressive in the workplace and more passive at home. This may be for a myriad of reasons, one being the lack of available Black men. Whereas in our workplace, we are unlikely to tolerate anything perceived as racist. Consequently, we are seen as "super strong" women.

Our Relationships

For Black Women Only...reflects the power and strength which comes from our heritage based on courage, creativity, and compassion. In my practice, Black women complain most frequently of: 1) not getting what they want out of relationships in which they function as heads of households and 2) lack of available Black partners.

The two are related in that if we do find an available man that is even halfway good to us, we tend to forget the times when he is not so good. We still don't make Black men responsible for their behavior, because we are still socialized to believe that having "half a man is better than none at all." We have all heard the saying: "It's a 50/50 thing." Right, we give 100 percent and they give 0 percent. Each partner should give 100 percent to make the relationship work. I remember interviewing a client, a single, struggling parent and never asking about the father of the child and his involvement or worse his responsibility to that child! Even I have become jaded to the absence of Black men in our world; as a result, we end up as heads of households--a lonely task in which we usually feel, and usually are, unsupported. Add a little societal disdain for our condition and you have the recipe for becoming disempowered; and that affects our relationships with our kids, friends, boyfriends, husbands, lovers, and it usually originates with our parents.

A reader says:

> "...Fear of womanhood and sexuality when I think of being abused as a teenager and child, watching my mother(s) be abused, and being abused in my own marriages, I don't want female responsibilities and roles. Additionally

harassed and abused on my job because after all isn't that what the traditional female role...represents?"...

Betty, 42, divorced,
nursing attendant, Pittsburgh.

Other relationships: Our mothers, fathers, sisters, brothers, friends, lovers, and children are like examined; topics such as "PARENTIFICATION," "SISTERIVALRY," and the "CYCLE OF MEN" are discussed as well. For example, the relationship with our mother is perceived as volatile--and usually is--because almost no Black woman is happy with her mother. We spend a lot of time trying to change their behavior which, of course, is impossible. I think of my own maternal relationship in that I wanted my mother to be as assertive and independent as I am (and went so far as to set her up in her own day care business). Predictably, my mother never followed through with my desire because that is not what she wanted to do. My work situation is not her work situation.

Our Work

For Black Women Only... examines the 40-hour hustle: The J-O-B--work. As we are such a varied race, we fit into four distinctive work groups: the "UNEMPLOYED, the UNDEREMPLOYED, the EMPLOYED, and the ENTREPRENEUR." We are a vital part of the work force and frequently feel unsupported. Different from White women, our history with work has been to protect ourselves, feed and clothe our children, and only recently, to satisfy us as individuals. Topics such as our "CRISIS-CENTERED LIFE-STYLE" and the "ABLE DISABLED" are covered here as well. One of the biggest problems I have seen in my practice is being the "ONLY ONE" in the workplace, which is a heavy burden. You are called upon to represent every minority opinion whether you know about it or not; there is a constant balancing act between your personal identity of being an African American woman and "member of the company"--difficult!

A contributor says:

"...Even though I graduated with a 3.5 average and scored in the upper half of the state boards, I did not get hired in any of the specialty areas I applied for, even though hospitals advertised for new graduates and would train. In fact, when I settled for applying for simple entrance positions in hospitals, I still didn't get hired. Nursing homes--where no one wants to work--is for "black people." Keeping a job - we can expect to have to work four to five times as hard as our white counterparts in order to keep a job. We can expect to do jobs that they don't want to do, and we can expect some of them to be lazy, late, and absent and never get fired. Super woman: maintain job, home, husband, and children, and be 'perfect' in all of her roles, to never complain..."

Haneefa, 35, nurse, Peoria.

Consequently, we spend a great deal of time in the workplace and usually get very little satisfaction out of it. I recall one client telling me, "I stay at my job, even if I hate it, because I get three weeks' vacation every year," that leaves her with 49 weeks to be unhappy and probably unproductive. Taking care of ourselves needs to become more of a priority--empowerment at all costs.

Empowerment for Everyone, Especially for Us

For Black Women Only... also provides insight into the "ABC's of our EMPOWERMENT." The whole concept of empowerment and feeling better about ourselves boils down to expressing our feelings, anger in particular (The A!), which is frequently unexpressed or expressed in an aggressive fashion. One client was so out of touch with her feelings she would watch many, many soap operas just to know how to react. "I was too afraid to let others know how I felt. I frequently felt like a teakettle that had boiled over on the back of the stove and then I felt guilty afterward, always guilty for being mad." We attempt to change or control everyone's behavior (The B!) except our own; as with my mother, it is impossible to change anyone's behavior except our own. Our self concept (The C!), unfortunately, is still largely determined by the media--White, of course. African American people watch more television than any other race, and what is reflected back to us are still largely White images we unconsciously view as correct, which naturally decreases our self-esteem and concept. During this writing, I frequently had the television on and the number of White images were, of course, pervasive. A local talk show described a "natural woman" as being one with no makeup and long, straight hair--obviously they've never heard of Aretha! I recall a colleague once telling me that a seven-year-old client of hers remembered Rosa Parks as giving up her seat to someone White. Research has recently shown that young children still choose a White doll as more intelligent and attractive than a Black one. Our children continue to have difficulties in their school situation because we develop relationships which reinforce our skills, not the other way around.

More Blacks, whether in teaching roles or on TV, reinforce our positive sense of self.

This section of the book further discusses the concepts of "COMBAT FATIGUE" and "EFFECTIVE CULTURAL SWITCHING." Combat fatigue exists as a result of African American women living and working in a predominantly White, male-oriented society. (Remember we were not supposed to survive!) As a result we may have symptoms of depression: helplessness, hopelessness, low self-esteem, low energy or stress, physical or psychological symptoms that preclude our functioning on a day-to-day basis. If we are in a relationship, or worse, in a bad relationship, this complicates the condition. It is important for Black women to attend to this area.

A contributor says:

> "...You asked me if I was in a crisis and I sarcastically said no, because when I first went to Southeastern (clinic), I was so depressed I could hardly move or care for myself. I thought about suicide or hurting myself often and no one believed me. Comparatively speaking, I'm not in crisis but I'm not OK. The needs I have mentioned to you on the phone go a lot deeper than simply relationships and discrimination. When I woke up this morning crying and acknowledged that there has been a knot in my stomach since Monday, I realized that I am far from being OK, just numb and surviving. The holidays are very hard for me. I lost my baby, my mother, and separated from my husband (later divorcing him) at this time of year. I don't have children. Loneliness is a big issue for me. There are two (actually three) cultural differences that I have never talked over with a therapist before because I didn't think a white therapist would understand, and I felt embarrassed airing dirty laundry, so to speak..."

> *Barbara, 40, divorced,*
> *engineer, Charlottesville.*

This contributor is not uncommon in my practice and simply needs to begin dealing with combat fatigue effectively. We can become fatigued when dealing with a predominately White culture while trying to maintain our Africentrism. An effective way of dealing with and overcoming "fatigue" is through "Cultural Switching." "Cultural Switching" is the ability to get what you want from a majority society without selling out--"knowing the system" and using it to your advantage. A Black client, a fashion editor, told me that while she doesn't have to read Essence Magazine, she does have to read Vogue without many Black images. Similarly, one of my favorite stories regarding this is: Once, while shopping with a White colleague, she stopped to buy makeup. She asked if I wanted to buy some as well; I informed her that my "brand" was not readily available. She didn't believe me, so I had to proceed going from counter to counter so she would understand that "Fashion Fair" and "Flori Roberts" are not in every store.

While I was writing this book, I met with incredible adversity mostly from the White media/publishing (even though there are 40 million of us with $300 billion to spend, we are not viewed as a viable minority) and from White women who felt that they should be included in the book. In fact, one of the most provocative arguments that I got into was with a friend of mine. She actually said I made this statement to make myself look good: "In the work situation white women historically have not had to work." Historically it has been Black women in the workplace much, much longer; and if you are just going to view it from slavery on, I think the argument becomes even more clear-cut. Frequently, historians will confuse slavery with immigration. While there were immigrants who came to this country and worked, they did so by choice. We were denied that choice when we were enslaved for 300 years, and we still are enslaved. I had to explain time and time again that we needed a book that was clearly targeted toward our work and our relationships. I even had one friend who insisted that I write a disclaimer or an apology to my White friends--I had to laugh at that. The other argument I got frequently regarding relationships was "White relationships and Black relationships are largely the same." Unfortunately, White women have forgotten that there is a larger population of White men (and our men) from which to choose. They are also more likely to leave a relationship that is not working out and get into another one than we are, simply because of the lack of available Black men. African American men are almost a vanishing breed, and the solution that some Black women have chosen is to hang on to her man. In fact, I have had Black women sit in my office and say things such as, "He is a pretty good father, goes to work every day, but he has this cocaine problem. I should be able to live with that, right?" A classic example is the case of the former mayor of Washington, D.C., Marion Barry. Despite the hoopla, Mr. Barry is a cocaine addict and forgiven by the Black community for this offense. A Black man is reinforced for his irresponsibility. In fact, the number of Black women who have become heads-of-households is presently around 80 percent. Further, the number of Black women in the workplace has gone up 33 percent to 56 percent in 1988. Black working mothers with children under 18 rose, from 2,900,000 in 1978 to 3,170,000 in 1988.

But back to the point, the book did get written. In the beginning I got a trickle of responses, in fact, my first letter included mostly "yes" or "no" answers. But then I began to get responses practically everyday with support from all spheres: radio, TV, but mostly by word-of-mouth, for that I am grateful. After my first national exposure the responses came flowing in from drug dealers, prostitutes, housewives and secretaries to CEO's, the unemployed, and entrepreneurs; they were married, single, divorced, and from all age groups. Many wanted to speak at length via telephone. Many individuals chose to answer the questions one by one sending in essentially a book themselves. Others chose one particular question and answered it at length. Most, however, chose to answer all of the questions to some degree. And did the answers vary! Some people included everything and some people were unwilling to tell anything. For example:

> "...my relationship with my father is good. It is still, however, distant. I was not raised with him in the home. I didn't understand his role...my relationship with my mother is okay. I am still intimidated by her. I feel insecure in her presence. She is very domineering...I get along well with my brothers and sisters...I have few friendships but they are good...my relationship with my boyfriend and my children is strained. My son and my boyfriend don't get along at all. There has even been a physical fight..."
>
> *Anonymous*

...and...

> "...Dear Ingrid, I have been scuffling this letter of yours around for months. There was also an article in last Sunday's paper. I want to cooperate with you but I have a problem. I very seldom think of the past. My parents are deceased, and I don't allow myself to think of them as dead; but occasionally I will have instant happy and enjoyable moments thinking back to my childhood life..."
>
> *Anna, Milwaukee*

While the former revealed everything, the latter I found quite touching even though she didn't want to reveal much.

...and most women were grateful!...

"...I am Sivon for short. I am 20 years old; I work and attend college, all on a full-time basis. I was interested in participating in your study because I have had problems with personal relationships in the past. I wanted to talk to somebody about them, but the only people that I trust enough to tell my problems to are the same people that I am having problems with. Your study is an opportunity for me to express my feelings to a real person without worrying that I will offend anyone..."

"...it helped me to be able to write this down in black and white..."

Anonymous

"...I look forward to seeing the finished product and am hopeful that my entry may benefit someone in some way. I can honestly say it's been beneficial for me to put some of my thoughts about the people most important to me down on paper..."

Anonymous

"...I would like to take this time to thank you for allowing me the opportunity to share my opinion with you, and thank you for your concern and consideration; I read the articles, they were great. I look forward to hearing more from you. My prayers and motivations are behind you all the way..."

Hattie, 38, Las Vegas

"...in an effort to be as honest as I could, I did my writing and put it down to reread at a later time to see if my feelings were the same...well basically they were..."

Iris, 59, Maryland

"...since receiving your letter and reading over what you wanted answered, I have had to pause and dig into the attic of my mind to pull out the skeletons that I have hidden there so that I could function and survive in this society..."

Anonymous

...and there are letters like this...

"...one thing I can tell you about prison life is that it is not a pretty picture, and if you had to do it you would only want to do it once in your life. However, I would cooperate with you if I knew there was also something in it for me. Life is not easy nor is it indispensable. When I am released I will need some financial help in order to get my business going. I will need finances to build an inventory. I am looking for investors for the money to be paid back on a percentage over a period of a couple of years. Can you help me?..."

Anonymous
Margaret, 34

...some women wanted to talk back to Sharahzad Ali *The Blackman's Guide to Understanding the Black Women*...

"...Sharahzad Ali's *A Blackman's Guide to Understanding the Black Woman* is a horrifying example of how we as Black women viciously turn on each other when we feel hopelessly frustrated, angered, and trapped by a system that demands our silence, ignorance and complacency. It is an example of self-hatred/destruction at its prime. I have no doubt that there are serious problems between Black men and women. There are tremendous barriers that have been created to keep the black family in eternal disarray and Black people from healing themselves. However, the platform Sharazad Ali used to voice her frustration is simply a modern day auction block to further exploit the new slaves of economic, political, social, and racial injustice..."

"...let's get this book on the shelves...what we really say, not the world according to Sharazad Ali..."

Anonymous

When it comes to Black women outlining their desire to learn about themselves, particularly regarding psychotherapy, I got a gambit of responses from "What is psychotherapy" and "I don't want to" to "yes."

"...I realized that my entire family, relatives included, were dysfunctional in a BIG way, I have been trying to have some of them get some kind of help. I promised myself that the buck stops here and no more passing on abusive ways to my children or their children. Needless to say, I am considered to be 'different' because I have chosen to do something about the sickness that has been my family's legacy to me. By getting therapy I am changing my legacy to my children. I have taken parenting classes, we have been to family counseling and my daughter and I are taking individual counseling. It is very hard to find counseling for children under 12 because someone out there is under the fallacy that you can't help a child unless he or she is a certain age. Prevention is better than fixing or healing..."

Anonymous

...and this anonymous response...

"...I have been in and out of therapy for quite a number of years, I feel that I still have not found the 'real me.' I think part of the problem is that I am culturally mixed (and mixed up!)..."

Most contributors thanked me for the opportunity to express their feelings in writing and said that it had been a rather cleansing experience. Many wanted to know if "Women Helping Women" (support groups) were available in their areas, or how to find a therapist.

Dear Sister,

"...though I have never met you, I would like to thank you for validating my experiences, feelings, and thoughts. My contribution is extremely minor and not noteworthy, but you have given me the opportunity to write about feelings that I have kept buried for most of my adult years..."

Anonymous

I particularly loved the letters that started at a particular time and ended at a particular time. One from 28-year-old Elene in Detroit began at 2:30 a.m., and ended at 5:30 a.m., which is actually my best time for writing as well. She described:

"...my pen is still burning; and I hope I've not provided too much information, but I felt a need to write. I hope it hasn't been in vain because for me writing is therapeutic...furthermore, I can use this when dealing with my own therapist..."

"...I have begun to work on taking control of my life. Reclaiming my life from alcohol, marijuana, cigarettes, and abusive relationships is very important to me. I've also begun to try to build my self-esteem. I don't blame my mother, but I feel that I'm a product of the way she raised me--this is a major reason I want to be a part of this self-help book..."

Anonymous

And sweetest of all, many women gave me more credit than I deserve.

"...your personal touch in writing this book is one that will always be remembered. I look forward to meeting you one day, and I if I am in Milwaukee I will try to phone and say hello. I mostly enjoyed reflecting upon the areas that you are including in the book and do hope that my response has helped you in making this one of your greatest works. I have just formulated a mentoring group for young-black women from ages 18 to 35. What is unique about these young ladies is that they are already successful black women and that makes it very special to me. Again, thanks so much for being one of those sisters who continues to make a difference in our lives..."

Majorie, Toledo

For Black Women Only: A Successful Guide to Life-Style Change--at last, help has arrived--you are going back to school.

Ingrid D. Hicks, Ph.D.

Women have to share their feelings with their mothers

CHAPTER 1

Mother:
How can I Stop Being Angry at Her?

>"In African American women, mothers come in two kinds:
the childhood mother and the adult mother."
>
>*Maya Angelou, author.*

The "CHILDHOOD MOTHER" provides nurturance from your scraped knee to your first broken date; the "ADULT MOTHER" teaches you life experience, responsibility and decision making. Unfortunately, you rarely get both "mothers in one" and, as a result, angry resentments occur and fester into adulthood. That is why we as Black women adopt other mothers or say she is my "second mother" or my "play mother." We are looking for what we feel we don't have. I found this chapter's letters most poignant, and clearly the one most unique to the African American experience:

>"...I was raised in a two-parent home by my mother and my maternal grandmother. Unfortunately, I was invisible to them. I felt that I was a 'good' child, but my older half sister was horribly mean to everyone. I remember her once slapping me for no reason. My mother never once intervened. She told me to figure it out myself. As I got older I became a 'schizophrenic militant,' acting for social change and dating White men--looking for the 'love' I never got as a child. I always felt that if my mother was more like 'June Cleaver' I would have turned out differently..."
>
>*Stephanie, 32, single,
student, Berkeley*

>"...My mother died at age 21, I was only six years old. I was raised by an old maid aunt, who died when I was 12. I was then raised by a stepmother who was 18 years older than I. She had received a degree from Wilberforce University in the '40s. She saw to it that I had the best of everything until I left home at age 18..."
>
>*Shirley, 48, divorced,
certification specialist, Detroit*

>"...Elizabeth is 87 years old. We have been friends a little more than a year now, but it feels more like she has been in my life always. I stayed with mother (Elizabeth) when I was healing from stress in my life. I was simply drained. Mother was the most wonderful thing to happen to me last year. Even when my "real" mother, Margaret, was in town, I would visit "mother" and share meals with her..."
>
>*Bernice, 28, engaged, director of youth ministry, Gary*

What's most notable in this set of letters is the whole concept of adult versus childhood mothers. What is also apparent is the pain that each of these women endured while trying to fill a void they felt was sorely missing. In Stephanie's example, she had an "adult" mother. If and when she becomes a mom, she will likely overcompensate and become a "child" mother, which will be great until her child is 12. Stephanie now has the chance to learn to be "both kinds of mothers" by learning to love herself.

In her poem "Phenomenal Woman," Maya Angelou talks about the specialness of womanhood, important for African American women who have had a lot of experiences in which they had to "grow up in a hurry." Stephanie, like many Black women, fills multiple roles: student, daughter, sister, and race representative.

She has not accepted herself as a person, which is the cause of her "schizophrenia" (more on schizophrenia in Chapter Nine 9). Because we are "natural" nurturers, we go to the end of the earth for anyone, particularly anyone related to us, as in Stephanie's case.

Shirley and Bernice talk about the difficulty in relating to their respective mothers and their desire to find another mother, either out of necessity or habit. All of these women feel as though there is a deficit in the relationships with their mothers and, thereby, deficits in all of their other relationships from that day forward. Most often this takes the form of subjugating our needs to take care of others--good, nice girls lovable to everyone except ourselves.

In *A Woman's Place* by Marita Golden, our desire for being responsible for many things is well outlined also. As one of her characters, Faith, says, "I'm a mother, the world depends on me." The label "good girls" applies to many of us. We believe that if we love someone enough they will love us back. Unfortunately, that is not true. We may even believe, as Stephanie did, that White men may treat us better than Black men who treat us poorly. For example, she has internalized the notion that she is unlovable and over-compensates by being extremely "nice"; she is hoping the nicer she is the more others will like her, which will never happen. Shirley and Bernice believe that as well. It is this "white quotient" (WQ) that is so harmful to us and our developing self-concept as a child.

A contributor from Kansas says:

> "...my mother is comparatively light--although I may be wrong, it seems to me that mom more easily accepts people if they are 'pretty', light, and have straight hair or have narrow/thin features. Unfortunately, I am brown and my

hair is nappy. I remember mom talking about how pretty two of my friends were when I was 12 or 13. Their beauty was mentioned again and again. I remember asking her one day, 'Do you think I am as pretty as...?' Mom looked at me without a smile and said, 'What do you think?' It still hurts a little knowing that when I could have used knowing that I was pretty in her eyes, she could not find it in herself to label me as such. I have made many mistakes with my own 17-year-old daughter, but I have always let her know that I think she is beautiful..."

Anonymous

and a 28-year-old teacher writes:

"...my mother has always described me as being like my father, and because she divorced him when I was five, I always felt emotionally abandoned by my mother...she said that my father was crazy and always depressed. Those are the exact words she used to describe me. She said that I was crazy because I shook my leg too much just like he did. She said that I was too moody and should always be 'nice'. Because I was a child, I believed what she told me and internalized her constant rejection of my looks-- unfortunately I looked like my father. To correct my 'problem' she would have me pinch my nose so, in her words, 'it wouldn't get any flatter than it already was.' She had me doing blowing exercises with my mouth (as if blowing bubbles) because she said the exercises would make my full lips thin. Thank God I have good hair. What I remember most was how I was always scared to do anything around my mother. I rarely practiced the flute at home, and only if I knew the composition perfectly. I was scared to tryout new recipes after once failing at making french toast. I remember in the seventh grade winning the school spelling bee but losing in the first round in county competition. As she drove us home, I was in tears. I would have given anything for her to say something nice to me. We rode home in silence, except for me gulping down my tears. At school, when elected to lead a club, such as the debate team, the Spanish club, or the year book feature section, I would always lie to the faculty advisor and make an excuse as to why I couldn't serve in the elected capacity. As I got older, the thought of being given any opportunity was seen as being given the chance to automatically fail. I was scared I would screw up and my mother would find out and not be surprised. That gross lack of confidence is an issue in my life today. I graduated from high school one year early and took with me, into the real world, all of my pain, fear, and denial. I was a quiet teenager, never dated and had few friends. I was an African American teen in an all white school system and not popular, though I was admired for being a 'smart girl and not like other Black people'..."

What saddens me is not only the relationship with their mothers is bad, but we perpetuate our own low self-image. I am particularly troubled by the "eurocentric" emphasis these 'mothers' have instilled in their children. African American women in particular have enough problems without being divisive. Good hair, bad hair, and light versus dark skin comparisons are simply unacceptable today. Dr. Jawanza Kunjufu, a noted educator, says that this reinforces the negative image White media already have of us. In fact it is a two-step circular process: White media denigrate us and then we in turn denigrate ourselves for not being White.

As a 28-year-old teacher described:

> "...I was scared I would screw up, and that my mother would find out and not be surprised..."

Imagine going through life thinking and believing that everything you touch is going to turn to coal. The precept for this woman began with her mother "whitewashing" her, living in a White neighborhood and participating in "eurocentric" activities while not being reinforced in respect to her African heritage. "I can't do anything right." We need to love ourselves as we are.

It may be that "Kansas" and the 28-year-old teacher had a similar experience, but it clearly is still affecting "teacher" adversely. "...that gross lack of confidence is an issue even today..." My guess is just as "teacher" was hesitant to try new things at school, such as the debate team or Spanish Club, it is the same today. She may even still believe that she is only acceptable the more "White" she is. This may include who she chooses as friends, in particular when she interacts with other African Americans, how she acts, what she wears, and where she lives. She, in effect, has gotten "lost."

One of the worst disservices we do to our children is move them into a White neighborhood. I remember growing up in Flint, Michigan, in an all Black neighborhood, our family physician lived next door to those who worked in the factory. When I was 11, my family was moved, by that infamous "urban renewal," into an all-White neighborhood where we were clearly not wanted. I lost sight of my cultural background and heritage and soon thereafter began to plan my escape. Unfortunately, it was not until ten years later, and the loss left indelible marks on my maturation.

Today, I believe strongly in living an Africentric life: dressing and decorating my environment reflective of my culture, interacting primarily with other African Americans, and doing business within our community. It is an empowering experience personally and for those I mentor in my neighborhood!

Mentoring and role modeling were natural in my black neighborhood; and many of us unfortunately, still believe we have truly made it when we move from the "hood." Nothing is further from the truth. What happens is we try to "get along" and develop this niceness, which only works at cross purposes. We can have a more positive impact on our youth if we stay put!

Many of the following chapters note groups and organizations that provide services for African Americans, but parenting and mothering is a learned skill best shared amongst us.

Further, I frequently tell "nice" women like "teacher" to continue to be nurturing but become more nurturing to yourselves so that others will nurture you. If you want to take care of other people for 23 hours a day, fine, but devote an hour to yourself calling it "self-time." You deserve it and your self-esteem will soar.

Not only does being nice mean nurturing yourself, it also means becoming angry even with those related to you, your mother included. Because we believe anger is a bad thing, it encourages us to look for "other mothers," those we won't be MAD at, or worse, feel guilty about. What needs to happen is that we get angry and accept it as an okay feeling. We may need to resolve these issues and express feelings of anger at our mothers.

> "...remember when I went to Eye Lab with you? I thought the insurance would cover my exam, or at least you would. But you didn't, and I ended up angry and frustrated. I got mad when I had to give Melanie (my sister) $5.00. I was trying to save money for college. I was buying all the stuff I could. Who bought the necessities Melanie needed? You did because Melanie could not keep a job. You never helped me like that, mom. Why did you never help me like that? I didn't get anything for my birthday last year. The year before last I got sheets, what will I get this year? Nothing, because I will be in Washington? I remember having to walk past the pop machine because I didn't have two quarters, but you were sending money for my sister's tuition and money for her to go to Burger King. That hurt like hell. Mommy...there have been times when I felt as though you were disappointed in me, not so much as what you said but the stuff you would do as well. You would take shots

talking about my hair, my body, and my skin and that was hurtful too. There have been things that I wanted to tell you and to talk to you about. I wanted your advice, but I was so afraid of what you would think or say I didn't know how to tell you, particularly that I was angry at you..."

Kelly, 25, single,
law student, New Haven

Kelly is furious with her mother; in fact, she has "stored up" several "angers" ("Eyelab...birthday..." so forth) until she is ready to blowup--unhealthy. Women have got to begin to talk about feelings that they have, when they have them, particularly with their mothers--especially anger. Internalizing it usually turns to depression and influences our relationships with everyone, particularly our kids. Without judging her mother (mothering is not a perfected skill), Kelly needs to express her feelings of what appears to be an emotionally abusive relationship with her mother. Getting it out will allow some healing to begin. Regardless of what her mother does, Kelly has to take responsibility for Kelly.

It is more difficult, but not impossible to do, when there is obvious sexual or emotional abuse present:

"...my relationship with my mother is strange. She always appeared to be jealous or envious of me. I don't know if I was misinterpreting it but there wasn't much support, and when the chips were down she didn't comfort me. She also gave me the 'I told you so' mode. I'll never forget the last year of college I had transferred from the University of Chicago to Columbia College to get my degree in advertising because it was closer to my home. After I left the University of Chicago, she swore that I wouldn't complete my education; that I would end up pregnant by some man. Another incident: I had just broken up with a man I had been dating for two-and-a-half years. I found out that he had gotten married to a woman with whom he had had a long-term relationship prior to our meeting. Mind you, he didn't tell me. I called my mother extremely upset and crying, and she didn't want to talk to me. She said that she would call me back. Two or three hours later, she returned my call and by that time I had composed myself. When I needed her just to say 'hey, it's not your fault,' she wasn't there for me. But she had told the entire family and her entire (no exaggeration) church congregation about it. She couldn't, or was unable, to comfort me..."

Anonymous, Missouri

"...the relationship with my mother is very strained at best. My mom has always told me that I was a mistake, and that it was my younger brother's father that she really loved. Therefore, much of her attention, praise, and outward affection was focused on my brother. There are the details of how she left me to be raised by her younger sister, and how she tried to leave me with a cousin and his wife, who could bear no children--all these hang as skeletons in our family closet. After she married my stepfather, she quickly became the target of his physical abuse. She would often involve my younger brother and me in their fights. So on several occasions, I was fighting my stepfather as her protector. Eventually, he also began sexual gestures toward me. After talking with my grandfather, he told her; and she refused to believe it. She called me a liar, and my grandfather refused to let me return home with her. She resented that I left and, therefore, did nothing else financially or emotionally for me. Fights followed by sex were the general rule that controlled their relationship. I became very independent and vowed never to be like, or live like her...I graduated from high school two months pregnant. My mother said that she wanted nothing to do with me, and said that she considered me dead. In fact, we didn't speak until my son was seven months old..."

Cordelia, 26, married,
child counselor, Milwaukee

"...I could never, and I believe ever, trust my mom; she has let me down so often in my life that I am afraid to trust her. The reason for this is my mother never provided me with security. About five times during the course of my life all of my belongings, my personal possessions as well as my bed, were taken away from me. My mom, my sister, my aunt, and I were evicted from our home. Mind you, this has happened on five occasions and from five different apartments. On one of these occasions, I had come home from school only to find all of my belongings on the street. My mom never satisfied my sister, my aunt, nor me with any explanations as to why our rent was not paid; and she never really has said that she is sorry. Needless to say, this has led to resentment toward my mother. Interspersed among these five evictions, my mother and I fought. All in all, life with my mother has been as unstable as the weather..."

Anonymous, Ohio

"...there is no 'real relationship' with my mother. I have never been able to communicate with her. She was always too 'tired,' and I was always too busy doing her job. She has found some way in her mind to blame me for most of the misfortunes of her life. She was abused by her father during most of her childhood; she took her feelings out on me from the day of my birth by using the same methods. After nearly two years of therapy, I have finally broken the emotional and self-abusive hold she has had on me for 41 of my 43 years of life. I got angry and left. I don't regret writing her off..."

Anonymous

Although anonymous, the pain of sexual and emotional abuse is significant in all of these letters. They may need to work through this pain through their faith, friends, or psychotherapy; but they need to get on with their lives. Not easy but very necessary. We need to resolve issues with our mothers.

Here searching for a "new mother" clearly is important, we may have to accept that we have "bad" mothers. Confronting the anger is the healthiest. We believe the old adage, blood is thicker than water, and because someone is related to us they will "do right" by us. People are people related or not.

For example, Cordelia clearly was sexually abused. "...I was a mistake...he (stepfather) began making sexual gestures toward me..." Moreover, in our family units it usually goes undiscovered because it is so common, or if we bother to tell someone, no one believes us. So we just take it, internalize the feelings and continue to self-destruct. In like fashion, "Anonymous Missouri" and "Anonymous Ohio" recount emotionally abusive situations with their mothers that are still unresolved. Missouri: "...she couldn't, or was unable to confront me..." Ohio: "...my mother was as unstable as the weather..." Both emotional and physical abuse are equally deadly and carry scars long into adulthood because it is related to our families--many times from mom. In order to progress in our lives successfully, we have to do the unthinkable--get MAD at mom.

Luckily, our last Anonymous contributor has done just that--gotten angry and gotten on with her life. ("I got angry and left, I don't regret writing her off...")

We need to keep ourselves surrounded by warm, supportive, nurturing relationships--whether they are family or the reinstitution of our traditional extended family. We can only benefit from such an arrangement. The following group of letters emphasizes the need for having a positive relationship with a mother figure--natural or chosen. Those that are successful in finding relationships are more successful in parenting and making the transition from childhood to adulthood and forging a relationship with their mother on a long-term basis.

> "...my mom was an English teacher and, to put it bluntly, she taught Marva Collins. I have always admired her for her professionalism and expertise in the classroom. In all the years I've been to school, not once did I ever hear a bad thing about my mother from any student. The worst I ever heard was 'Man, your mother sure makes you do a

lot of work.' Then a few years later when the same student came to visit, 'Your mother's class was the hardest, but it was the best I had.' When I reached high school, I was terrified to see on my schedule my mom for English. I think we ran into each other on the way to the principal's office to change the schedule to someone else. It was the worst mistake I ever made as far as school was concerned. My mom also had a strong devotion to family and a commitment to church that was as strong. She was involved in more community things than I can count, and yet she always had a dinner for us everyday from scratch. She is the best cook that I know of and great with cakes...even though our relationship has had its ups and downs, the one point in my life that marked the turn in our relationship is one summer day on a Sunday. I was dressing my youngest for mass, he was eight months old, and I was four months pregnant with my son Allen. Suddenly it all just seemed too much. I hadn't cried or anything and I guess, like my mom, just decided in my mind to deal with it. But at that time my other side caved in, and I put the baby down and just cried. My mom came from upstairs and put her hand on my shoulder and she said, 'Karen, you just have to keep going, honey. Everyone makes mistakes. But no matter what you just put your head up and carry yourself well. Don't give anyone the chance to say their talk has beaten you down.' I looked up and saw not just my mother but a friend..."

Karen, Chicago

"...my mother and I are very close. We talk daily about any and every subject. She is my friend, guide, mentor, counselor, my doctor, shrink, preacher, teacher and always my mother..."

**Pamela, 32, divorced,
UPS clerk, Warrensville Heights**

These mothers (particularly in the first letter "...my mom taught Marva Collins...) were able to adapt to their daughters becoming adults, and they have a much easier time developing and forging positive relationships on a long-term adult basis. It's the development of a "friendship" with a mother figure that is important. "Karen" discovered that, and even her "supermom" accepted her (as I've said mothering is not a perfected science, we cannot all make piecrusts and run a class in the same day--don't hold yourself to unreasonable standards) which helped her accept herself.

There are, however, some relationships that are symbiotic; that is, a situation where children do not merge into adults such as the following account.

"...my mother and I are good friends and great roommates. I have lived with her since she and my father divorced, and she moved (with me in tow) to California. I am 34 and she is 62. What is really terrific is that we get along great, and we support each other financially and emotionally. We have other relatives. However, they live in different states; and we have never been very close. We do write sometimes; and they sometimes answer, but no close ties. As a result of this, we depend on each other. We feel we have no one else. My mother and I do not date, so we enjoy a social life together. We always have someone to go out with. We are both independent and dependent on each other. She handles all the things that I don't; and I, all the things she doesn't. We share life expenses. I don't see any benefit to our living separate lives. We get along extremely well, and we both feel that our lives are much richer together than if we were apart..."

Patricia, 34, single,
Beverly Hills

While this situation sounds comforting, Patricia has not evolved into an adult or developed other relationships (in fact, she's written them off "...my mother and I do not date, so we enjoy a social life together...") away from her mother. While usually more apparent in our male children (see Chapter four), it's present here. Our family units tend not to mature and move out on their own. It is not unusual for 29- and 30-year-old children to still be living at home rent and responsibility free. We, in fact, are reinforcing their irresponsibility. We need to realize we are raising someone else's husband or wife, hopefully responsibly. The following poem probably best illustrates what kind of relationship we as African American women would like to have with our mothers.

MOTHER TO DAUGHTER

The miracle of your birth
Gave meaning to my life
Don't go astray
Or be misled
Don't look back on your life
Then wish you were dead
Keep strong my child
Always be beautiful
Make education your goal
And success your style
Pick wisely your friends
You don't want to be hurt
Watch out for slick men
Keep away from dirt
I love you little flower
You are indeed my dear
Whenever you get into trouble
Know always mom is here

Wanda, 35, single,
office assistant, Jamaica, NY

We all can be better mothers and daughters!

THE 1-2-3 OF IT

We need to:

1. Know that being angry at our mothers and loving ourselves (in any color) are both okay. It is okay to express anger in particular without feeling guilty even at mom.

2. Resolve issues with our mothers through faith, family, friends, or psychotherapy (see Chapter 12) particularly if we feel emotionally abused or have a history of past physical abuse.

3. Develop a positive relationship with our extended family or our "second mother," particularly if the above applies.

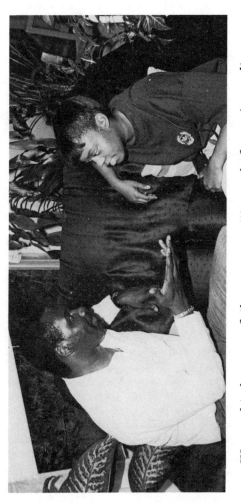

We need to have our fathers or a positive male figure in our lives.

CHAPTER 2

Fathers:
How Can I Stop Feeling Abandoned?

"My father had scared them to death. I think it was the first time a black man had ever come into Louis B. Mayer's office and said, "I don't want my daughter in this mess." Lena Horne, singer.

Our fathers represent our first "heterosexual" relationship. Consequently, like Lena, many Black women are eager to please their fathers (daddy's girls), which "colors" future choices of male partners. Because Black men are frequently absent in our family unit, absentee fathers represent, in African American women's minds, absentee men--which we'll do anything to keep, (developing into the "CYCLE OF MEN," more on that later) and this only hurts us. This chapter, next to chapter Six (another man chapter!), had the most responses, and women answered this question, if no other.

Contributors replied:

"...my biological father abandoned me and my mother when I was three years old. He remarried and had two other daughters. Throughout my childhood, he was 'flaky and irresponsible' and, most importantly, rarely present. He would surface every few years with his charming smile, beautiful diction, accentuated by his Northern accent. He would be impeccably dressed in his finest suit and slick new 'rented' car. All my life I heard...'your daddy ain't shit'...I would cry and defend my father because all my childhood memories of him were the 'great fun-loving times' we had when we were together..."

Anonymous

"...left on my sixth birthday prior to the cutting of my birthday cake. This leaving so overwhelmed my six-year-old senses, I have no memory of this event. My father probably loves me, but loves freedom and women more..."

Anonymous

"...my father and mother separated when I was 11 years old, and then divorced when I was 13. I love him because he is my father, but I do not love and respect him as a man. He does not know what responsibility is, and therefore he is not a responsible adult. He knows nothing about raising children, because he never really had the full responsibility of taking care of his children on a long-term basis. He thinks material things make up for love, but they don't. He has shown me through his actions what I don't want in a man, and to never fully depend on a man, be it a father, a lover, or a husband. I have a lot of anger toward him that I am beginning to let go of, but I am hoping that one day he will wake up and realize what it means to be a 'daddy'..."

Anonymous

"...I met my father for the first time at the age of 15. I remember him saying he was ashamed for me to meet his wife and their three children. His rationale for this feeling was that he did not want his wife to know he had a daughter as old as I was. Before I left his life, he told me that I had no reason to feel special because I had brothers and sisters all over the world. My papa truly was a 'rollin stone'..."

Anonymous

Even anonymous, all of these women were separated from their fathers in one way or another, but more importantly, they feel abandoned. Whether they are forsaken through "divorce, remarriage, or after the cutting of a cake," abandonment leads to feelings that they are responsible for their fathers leaving and somehow not good enough for them to stick around for, thereby creating or re-creating low self-esteem. Again, taking responsibility for something that is not ours, we continue to do it to our disadvantage. The following set of letters, describe the flip side of this problem: being a daddy's girl--women who have high expectations of themselves and low expectations of the men in their lives. Consequently, if we make a mistake--even a tiny one--we are unworthy of love from others or ourselves. Both lead to what we will later discuss as the "CYCLE OF MEN."

"...admittedly, I am a daddy's girl, and I could not tell you why. I am still struggling with that part of myself. He truly believes the sun rises and sets three inches from the back of my head. We have a 'good' relationship and talk about most anything. I am just beginning to feel 'free' of his expectations I have imposed on myself. I realize that he just wants me to be happy and successful. Daddy really treated mother poorly, and I still have a problem with that. He has always been busy and remains so to this day, but I can usually reach him somehow. My son goes to church with him so we do see him. I have received some strange signals about relationships by watching my parents; my past tragically reflects it. Who do you blame and how do you forgive? How do you not love someone who will take his head off and give it to you...?"

Jeaneen, 41, married,
housewife, Detroit

"...the relationship with my father is strained. He is a perfectionist. To him, I was stupid as a little girl; I imagine that I still am as an adult. As I was growing up, I was known as 'one of the Cheetum twins.' I was told and can remember that I followed my father around when I was young as he went about his work at the hotel in the bar downstairs. My father was also a stranger to me. I didn't know him even though I spent the first 11 years of my life in the same house with him. As a child I went fishing with him a few times and to the drive-in once. Besides the $20 he gave my mother every week for food and all other expenses including our clothes, I can only remember my father giving me a white panda bear and a doll during my entire life. I have no memories of climbing into his lap to cuddle or being hugged by him. He did none of the things that fathers do. The memories of my father that stand out in my mind are few. One that comes to mind is of him leaving dressed up on a Saturday night hot and steamy; tub dirty full of grit and grease, dark suit, white cashmere coat (double-breasted) with hat creased just so in the middle to match. I knew he would be gone for several days; most likely out with one of his women, drinking and gambling until his money was gone...I always wanted my father to be what he wasn't--a father to me. I always was longing to love him no matter what..."

Barbara, 61, married,
alcohol and drug counselor, Miami

Jeaneen was a daddy's girl and Barbara "wanted to be" a "daddy's girl," and like our first set of anonymous letters, all struggle with their self-image even today. Their self-worth, or lack of, has depended on their fathers' behavior (particularly Barbara), which was deplorable--but accepted. Clearly they were emotionally abused. More importantly, African American women are frequently abused, but it goes unreported. Unreported because in our community we are encouraged to take a more passive role in relationships to hold on to that all-elusive male. This ideology is reinforced by our community (what goes on in the family stays in the family), and the fact that African American women have fewer financial resources than White women to get out of a bad situation. The courts also are not sympathetic. We need to understand men (fathers) don't abandon us, we allow them to misuse us. In any case, it begins what we'll call the "CYCLE OF MEN" problem as 27-year-old Denise from Illinois outlines:

"...when he wasn't working he, was out getting drunk. Therefore, much of the family activity didn't include him. We'd go to my grandmother's home, which indicated that my father was being physically and verbally abusive. The minute my brothers and I heard the shouting, we would automatically wake up and begin packing our clothes. This routine was performed with little objection or emotion. Many times, my father would become particularly abusive toward my mother and legal intervention would be required. Because my father would pull the telephone out of the wall, I would walk to our neighbor's house next door. The neighbors would instantly know what I wanted, since the shouting would have awakened their family as well. I would stand there crying until the police came, who would say there was nothing they could do since my father was 'the man of the house'. Consequently, the three significant relationships I have shared with men are 1) a man 15 years my senior who I worked for when I was 15, 2) a man I met in college and dated for over five years, and 3) the man I married. Man Number 1 took me from jeans to expensive dresses and bought me after two years of 'gamming.' I thought if a woman had less than $50.00 in her purse, she was broke. After two year of showering attention and money on me, we slept together, and he taught me 'how to love a man.' Right after that I found that he was married and had been the whole time...Man Number 2 was a highly emotional love affair. The sight, smell, and shoulders of him gave me goose pimples; and we made love every night. Man Number 2 was my dream personified--handsome, intelligent, refined, and affectionate. I easily overlooked the occasional beatings that I endured for three years. I simply mentally 'checked out' and went limp when his emotions flared up...after the beatings he would be particularly affectionate and loving. I feared leaving him; thinking I could do no better. Finally, after some rather severe beatings, I confided in a friend and plotted to break the spell he had cast over me. My friend gave me strength by threatening to tell the world of his treatment toward me if I married him. The final straw occurred one evening while we were driving to a friend's graduation, he slapped me causing my lip to swell, he felt that I had 'talked back'. I jumped out of the car and out of the relationship...Man Number 3 was never my type though he was opposite of Man Number 2 in every way. He was cool, arrogant, and a ladies man. He was at least ten years older than I and had experienced at least 100 other women. Two months after our meeting, he gave me herpes for my 25th birthday. I accepted his proposal of marriage in the spring, accepting the fact that I could never have a relationship with anyone else now, and was married. Even though I knew I wasn't in love, nor did I find him attractive or sexually appealing, but I remembered what my mother told me when I asked her why she married my father. She responded, 'I believed I could grow to love him...''

As this particularly poignant letter establishes, in the African American family unit our male parent is frequently absent from the household; and we grow up feeling abandoned and consequently trying to rectify that. All of these women note what many Black women feel: ALONE. In dealing with what I call the underlying "CYCLE OF MEN" problem (no man, that man, any man), we will do anything to keep a man--even a bad one--that is not healthy. Many Black women believe "all men are dogs," and that this treatment must be endured. We feel that we lost our first man (father), which probably contributes to our feeling manless today. (My relationship with my father somewhat mirrored Denise's until I smartened up. My father was emotionally abusive, I didn't deserve it and quit taking abuse from him, and men like him.) Denise's letter is particularly painful because she still idolizes her father and looks to replace him over and over again--meaning being abused over and over again--as her letter describes...(man #1, man #2, man #3...). That is where the "CYCLE OF MEN" comes into play: we get burned by a guy (we've all been there), if he could just l-o-v-e me, if he would just be more responsible... more decisive...make a commitment...change...if...I'm going to leave him and we do. Then we go out, don't get on with our lives, feel lonely, and choose someone of the same ilk (any man). Get abused again and believe we were better off with the first guy (that man). We feel locked into bad relationships--but forget we have the key. We are always in complete control--but we don't believe it and consequently stay in a bad situation. Another variation of this problem is that we believe if only we could love them enough, work the right job, raise the right kids, cook the right food, and be sexy enough in the bedroom, all would be right: they would straighten up and give us the things we need. Wrong, wrong, wrong. We need to understand our self-worth depends on us.

Part of our problem, of course, is that we still give our control away to men. We must learn to demand and expect more from them. In fact, we have "loved them too much" and, consequently, not made them responsible for their behavior. Until we do so, I suspect we need to reclaim the concept of the extended family, relying on each other to reestablish these relationships within our community. In Marita Golden's, *Long-Distance Life* such a community is established. There should be no rules for how the Black family unit is set up. By reclaiming our experiences, the "extended family" can provide more positive role models for our kids; and we are ultimately happier, which is, in fact, what many authors including Marita Golden outline.

"...you men are all alike, mama laughed. Think that you can make us feel, whether it is in our heart or between our legs, it is a most important thing. And then when the feeling is gone, you go start it up with somebody new..."

In the story, Faith and Charles had wanted to get married. Faith's mother didn't condone it and was telling her daughter that her life was going to end up very much like hers. In fact, Faith's mother still harbored old resentments toward her husband. Faith and her mother argue, "...and it is my daddy she hates too...the daddy you wouldn't even know if you passed him on the street...the daddy I love anyway...the daddy I'll never forgive..." Her mother continues "Get you some education and you won't need no man. A degree will never let you down. A college education won't get up in the middle of the night, hit the door and be gone forever. Nobody ever regretted having an education. I know plenty of women regretted having some man or other in their lives..."

Similarly, Cheryl Lee summarizes the pain that we feel and will continue to feel, until we take charge of our lives!

"My mother my father and I
equal a triangle, you see.
There is no way out of a triangle,
because you are locked in
there is no key.
Since nine years old,
I've been locked in a triangle
which was introduced to me
at an age that sets the stage
for my life drama of pain
to reveal my pain is to heal me,
to release my parents,
to live,
to inspire others to live,
but I seem to have lost
my desire to live."

Where then do we begin to repair our relationships with our "fathers" so to speak? By concentrating on the positive--that is, the good things we remember. We can build on these and help one another make the changes we need to make, and expect more from them. As with "mothering" this too needs no "organization" or group--it is and can be up to us.

Like:

"...as I began to read over the questions, I decided to answer the first one. As a matter of fact, the questions really hit home because, I believe, many black women really do not discuss their relationship with their fathers...especially when they are young or, in most cases, have only seen negative points about their fathers...but my case is so unique. My relationship with my father was one of the best male relationships I have ever had. My father was an army man, but he always worked two jobs. When he was not working he still always found time for my sister and two brothers, as well as for me. He used to go to the carnival and bring home stuffed toys, hot dogs, and always had a smile on his face. He gave me so much love and affection. Sometimes I think he gave me too much. It seems to me now, as an adult that I look for the same affection in my relationships. I look for attention, affection, and most of the time do not receive it. Most black males never got it, so they in turn do not know how to give it...In my relationships, I look for strength because my father had a lot. Everything my father had that was positive I tried to find in my relationships."

Anonymous

"...I hope the enclosed will be of help to you because I think the relationship between me and my parents was great. But I chose my father because I feel this is my way to honor him, since his passing. My father gave me life skills by showing me how to write checks and fill out applications when I was only nine years old. He held a black history session on Saturdays for my brothers and me as well as taught me to enjoy reading by taking me to the library at an early age. He made me have pride in myself and told me there wasn't anything I couldn't do. Consequently, my father molded me to be independent, loving, and considerate..."

*Margaret, 40, divorced, grandmother,
team leader at a blood service, Richmond*

"...the most important lesson my dad taught me on the nights we would talk on my balcony was the order of priorities. They were: God first, family second, me third, and everyone else after. After that I began to remember some of the things that my father had done for me over the years..."

*Karen, 28, married,
secretary, San Francisco*

"...my father often remarked that I was the best 'boy' he had...even though I had three brothers and one sister. I am the youngest of five children. At an early age, I learned to ride horses bareback (dreaming I was like Annie Oakley). We are black, but in my geographic area we never heard of any famous black people and, therefore, had no mentors except for the teachers. I suppose because many of them rented rooms and boarded at our house, I had just about enough of them. I recall the smell, after they left the bathroom, of Lysol baths and Tabu or Old Spice fragrances. I'd rather smell leather saddles and barnyard stench...Each Labor Day, we had to scrub and groom our horses for the parade, and my sister and I had our own little surrey decorated to a 'T' and our Western attire labeled simply the 'Gibson Girls.' We always rode behind dad and his prancing Tennessee walker, and of course, we rightfully took home many blue ribbons and prizes because we had the best, not because we were black..."

Anonymous, Tennessee

"...my father died when I was nine years old, he nonetheless had a profound influence on my intellectual, political, and cultural development. We spent many hours talking about history, jazz, and current events. I credit him with my pursuit of the intellectual life, my love of jazz, and my political orientation..."

Sarah, Bryn Mawr

All of these women, particularly Margaret, Karen and Sarah, have strong positive memories of their fathers, which served as building blocks for their future relationships with men. Life skills, such as writing checks, prioritizing life: "...God first, family second, me third...", and the development of self-esteem are evident. "...I was the best boy he had..." Even in the worst situations, we can still find something positive to recall and that's where we should begin to build. We need to have positive male figures in our lives and we can if we have high expectations of them.

THE 1-2-3 OF IT

We need to:

1. Understand that men, including our fathers, don't abandon us; we let them misuse us and this depletes our self-esteem. We keep asking what have we done wrong? The correct answer is nothing.

2. Understand our self-worth is dependent on us--not on what our fathers or other men expect. Regardless of whatever relationship we are in we contribute wholly to it. As with our mothers, if we are not being treated right, we should get out! Emotional/sexual abuse is not acceptable. There is no such thing as a daddy's girl. We are now grown women, who are responsible for ourselves.

3. Begin building male relationships in the positive not the negative. We can't right their wrongs. There is no excuse for bad behavior. We want to duplicate this in all of our male relationships. Expect the best because we deserve the best.

Chapter 3

Sisterhood:
How can I Stop
Competing with my "Sisters?"

Part of my passion with Black women is that those who become achievers tend not to be involved in movements. White males tend to bond gloriously when they are accomplished, not us, we tend to go under the rug: compete, disappear, hide. We have got to bring glory along with us--a generation of Black women who are going to confront 21st Century realities. Jewell Jackson-McCabe, president, National Coalition of Black Women.

Even Alice Walker, in her book *The Color Purple* realized that the sisterhood means much more than blood lines. Celie and Nettie had a relationship that time and distance could not destroy. In their story, these sisters were raised by an abusive father. Celie then married an abusive man, who separated her from Nettie for years. Their only connection was from letters that Nettie wrote to Celie, which Celie discovered years later. Luckily they remained bonded.

Consequently, I believe that the relationships that we develop with our sisters provide the basis for the relationships we develop with women in later life. I compare the relationship I have with my "younger" sister Jill (very close) and my "older" sister Kimberly (not as close as I would like.); the relationships with women friends whom I'm close to have been patterned after my relationship with Jill. I think the difference comes from time spent together, and that we are similar. A close friend of mine, Quincy, talks about how she developed good relationships with her nine sisters. She thinks it's because they were all told they had special skills: "...one was designated as an expert cook and another an expert gardener. We never felt competitive. In fact, we had a group of ready-made problem solvers always available to us..."

Unfortunately, many of us have a terrible history and habit of competing with our natural sisters, which makes us compete with them in other arenas. We fought with them over men, in the workplace, and have been known to side with one another against each other--all to our downfall. Many times we don't recognize what I like to call "SISTERIVALRY" because it is masked and supported by other family members, particularly if one sister is doing well and living a proactive life and the other is not. Phrases like "she has forgotten where she came from" or "she thinks she is better than us" indicates this phenomenon. It is only when we support one another that any of us truly win and excel. When we realize a good bond with a "sister," natural or chosen, (many times we choose a close friend or other relative as a sister) it makes life worth living.

This chapter's letters demonstrate the better the bond with our natural (or chosen) "sisters," the better our relationships with women in later life.

> "...I am three years younger than my sister and whenever I try to have a heart-to-heart talk with her, she assumes the "big-sister" role. I am always wrong. I don't know anything. She is better than me because she has four children to my one. About 15 years ago my sister admitted that she never liked me because she thought I was better than her. I always wanted a big sister. I never had one. Even today, my sister is closer to friends than she is to me. When my son was past the diaper stage I was still trying to please my sister by driving to a special place just to buy diapers for her babies...what I remember most was the difference that was made between my sister and myself. There are several pictures of my sister as a baby; there is only one small faded picture of me..."
>
> ***Anonymous***

Our (Younger sister) contributor traces where her "SISTERIVALRY" began. "...what I remember most was the difference that was made between my sister and myself. There are several pictures of my sister as a baby; there is only one small faded picture of me..." The rivalry comes through when her sister tells her that she never really liked her--because she thought she (younger sister) was better than her. "Younger sister" continues to reinforce this behavior by comparing how many children they have respectively to what kind of diapers they wear. This probably has had an impact on her relationships with other women: "...I am always wrong...I don't know anything...," no one is always wrong. Everybody knows something. Her self-esteem is suffering as a result of her interaction with her sister. "Younger sister" needs to recognize "SISTERIVALRY" as these contributors outline:

> "...my sister Debra seeks shelter in her religion and, more importantly, away from me. We grew up close, then she joined a Pentecostal Church and threw me, jeans, and movies out the door. She is close to my mother which bothers me. It makes me angry actually. Even though I am more successful--well educated and have a good job--she is more respected by my mom...and it seems just about everybody else..."
>
> ***Donna, 38, married, computer technician, Nashville***

"...I guess I consider my first cousin sort a sister. We grew up next door to each other. I am the older by two or three years. As children we loved each other very much and were inseparable. I graduated college first, so naturally it was expected of me to help her get through as well. I did so willingly and generously. She went on to medical school, and I continued to help out. I was proud to be a part of her climb to the top. Later, as she eased into her role as a successful physician, she excluded me or rarely had time for me. The only time I hear from her is when she is going through an emotional low such as a divorce, or when she has 'boyfriend' problems because the details are much too intimate to share with her 'good time' friends. Often my honesty alienates us. So this last time we were sharing things, I asked her what kind of friend she wanted me to be...one that would be honest and tell her the truth or one that would tell her what she wanted to hear...she hasn't returned my calls since..."

Sheryl, 39, widowed,
data processor, Houston

This set of letters underscores what results from older sister and younger sister "SISTERIVALRY." Donna first talks about this between her and her younger sister. She says, "Even though I am more successful--well educated and have a good job--she is more respected by my mom...and it seems everybody else..." Her family unit, namely her mother, makes Donna feel guilty because she is successful. Unfortunately, she continues to compare herself to her sister, rather than ascribing to her wants and desires. Donna, if she continues in this vein, will begin to downscale her goals, perhaps even throwing jeans and movies out the window as well.

A similar situation exists for Sheryl. As an "older" sister she watched her sister enter and excel in medical school--while that was difficult enough--she supported her and now feels unappreciated for doing so. Her sister in turn has gotten angry and her noncommunication has separated them even further. The problem with both situations is that it circumvents us from excelling in our own lives. This is particularly evident in Sheryl's situation, "I graduated from college first, so naturally I was expected to help my sister...I did so willingly and generously..." two points: 1) She was not or should not have been functioning as a parental figure just because she was older--we frequently do that. Her parents should have provided support for her sister. 2) She did so willingly--but probably expected to be paid back. As with other relationships, they must function on an equal basis, this one clearly has not and so, Sheryl is angry.

Both Sheryl and Donna have lowered their expectations of themselves. Excel in your life despite familial pressures not to. Perhaps Donna will not become all she can be, she should. Perhaps Sheryl wanted to be a physician--she should and still can if she stops fighting with her sister, at home and in the workplace.

> "...I see many black sisters in key upper-level management positions and they work to appease white management instead of helping highly qualified blacks who have proven themselves beyond a reasonable doubt..."
>
> *Paula, 40, single,*
> *Realty Specialist, Clarksdale*

> "...at this time I'm not real sure, but there appears to be a communication breakdown. I am working with another black female and a Romanian female. We all have very strong personalities and that can make for an uncomfortable situation at times. I am the lead secretary, or the senior secretary, and I feel that there is a great deal of dissention and resentment. I find this disturbing and a little unnerving. However, I find the strength and confidence to deal with the matter and not let it overcome me. The resentment is not from the Romanian, it is from my so called "sister." Can you figure this?..."
>
> *Juanita, 32, married,*
> *senior secretary, Waldorf*

> "...my supervisor is a black woman in her 40's. She helps me a lot, but mostly she has hindered me. It seems that whenever she gets a chance she gets smart and loud with me. She does this with many people in our group because she knows we won't do anything. It seems to me that if you are quiet you get harassed; if not, no one will bother you. I am surprised it is from someone black though!..."
>
> *Maya, 25, nurse,*
> *single, Philadelphia*

Many organizations, such as the one Jewell Jackson-McCabe mentioned at the beginning of the chapter talks, about bonding through sisterly support. African American sororities such as ALPHA KAPPA ALPHA or DELTA SIGMA THETA (see "Resources") support the same notion. We simply underutilize them.

However, Paula, Juanita, and Maya, all have the same problem--old "SISTERIVALRY," which has reasserted itself in the work situation. Juanita points it out well, "I am the lead secretary..." setting herself up to fight with her sisterworker. Paula points out a similar problem. Many of us expect in the managerial situation that race is the only factor in promotions and raises. A combination of the worst case scenarios might be: if we have a Black boss we expect favors as a result, for example, arriving on COLORED PEOPLE TIME (CPT), or worse, we may not speak to the Black cleaning lady, both of which are totally unacceptable. Both situations are highly charged and probably result from earlier experiences with our sisters--as in our first set of letters.

Maya has the same complaint but her situation is complicated because it sounds as if she has not asserted herself with her boss (more on that in Chapter 11) as well. Maya clearly needs to tell her boss that this behavior is not acceptable. We need to support one another at work, particularly because we both win in the end.

We can develop positive sisterly relationships--mostly through increased communication with our older, younger, "adopted," or work sisters. Working through our problems via talking is a good place to start. Juanita and Maya can benefit from such a solution. In fact, the sooner the better, before their work situation becomes even more explosive. It may require something as simplistic as bringing in a superior to resolve their differences but may be as complex as being reassigned to another work area. In any case, a change has to be made for everyone's benefit.

Donna, and Sheryl but particularly "Anonymous," need to resolve their earlier "sister" differences, hopefully with a positive result. Digging up and resolving the "hurts" may be as simple as going to our "sister," but may require a family quorum. If not, a trip to the therapist is not inconsistent with repairing old hurts. Talking does help! Healing past ills is just the beginning. The ending is the progression of our lives.

> "...my sister Diana is five years older than I. Actually, she is my half sister; we have the same father, but her mother was his second wife and mine, his third. I saw her as my only sister, and I loved her dearly. I think the greatest compliment I have ever received came from a relative who made a comment to the effect that we acted like 'real sisters.' (I wondered at the time what else there was. Of course, we were 'real' sisters.) Not having a mother in common was not an issue, nothing we even gave a thought to. I was one of those little sisters who looked up to her big sister with nothing but admiration and love...I found I loved watching her brush her hair and the way it curled from being brushed softly around her face. She had an aura about her, things were different as soon as she entered a room. I suppose I should have been jealous, but I wasn't. I admired her so much that it seemed immaterial that everyone else did

also. As we grew up, we shared secrets about the men in our respective lives and gave each other advice. We would sit up all night talking. She gave and shared all her wisdom on pregnancy and childbirth with me. And it was as things should be--knowledge flowing from one woman to another. I heard it said once that only a woman can teach another woman how to be a mother. She lived here for about a year, became involved in a relationship which didn't work and decided to move on. She was always moving and never seemed to be able to settle down. We saw a lot of each other that year, laughing, talking, being connected--two kindred spirits very much in sync. After she left we wrote and ran up outrageous phone bills to stay in touch. I missed her very much. I visited her about a year later, and she was living in a high-rise in the worst possible part of town. I thought we were in trouble when the cab driver left us at the curb, after dumping our bags on the ground next to us. One good look around and I was almost tempted to call the taxi back, but it had already disappeared. All the stories I had ever heard about ghettos, gangs, etc., came rushing back. We prayed the elevator would work. The stairs looked too foreboding, besides she lived on the top floor. When we reached her apartment it took almost five minutes to open the door because of the number of locks she had. The next few days went by fast, and it was good to see her and that she was doing all right. Another time I saw her was when we went home for our father's funeral in May of 1978. At the funeral she walked up next to me and looked at our father and put her arm around me. The last time I actually laid eyes on her was July of the next year; she left home to go to the doctor and never returned. Nothing more was ever discovered about her disappearance to my knowledge. Sometimes I believe that she is still alive somewhere. Other times I am convinced that she is dead. She was having a lot of problems with an ex-boyfriend at the time. He was breaking into her house stealing and doing lots of crazy things. It is possible that he harmed her. It is a terrible thing not to know if she is alive or dead. I think of her almost daily, even after all these years. I still hear the sound of her voice, her laughter, and the way she would talk...there is still so much to tell her, I still need her advice on so many things..."

Elaine, 30, married,
sales rep, Missouri

Elaine clearly shared a sweet, poignant relationship with her sister which shows our capacity as African American women to gain so much from one another. Because I am an incurable romantic, I believe like Celie and Nettie, Elaine and her sister will be reunited. Because of their deep bond, Elaine has probably developed close, healthy relationships with other women. Remember sisters are special!

THE 1-2-3 OF IT

We need to:

1. Recognize "SISTERIVALRY" (e.g., "she thinks she is better than me"). The first step is recognition both from our natural sister and our sisterworker.

2. Excel in life despite the familial pressure not to, (e.g., "She has forgotten where she came from.") We shouldn't bow out of life because our families have chosen to--we can be the best we can be.

3. Support one another, particularly at work (certainly don't fight over men--any man--the man benefits not us). Many organizations (e.g., sororities) that are work related provide us with sisterly support.

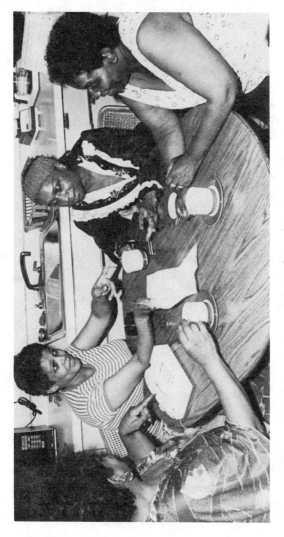

You are blessed when you have friends you can trust with your innermost secrets.

CHAPTER 4

Brothers:
How not to Fight With the Boys!

> "I grew up with three older brothers. My father made sure they allowed me to play on a ball team. I had to be not just good but extra good because I was a girl. A lot of times that's the first thing the guys would say, 'we don't want a girl on our team.' My brothers would say, 'that's okay, we'll take her.' Next time we would go play I was the first chosen."
>
> **Wyomia Tyus, athlete.**

Two problems exist with our "brothers." First, at home, we as children compete for attention from our parental figure. Noted lecturer, Dr. Kunjufu states that our mothers tend to love their sons and raise their daughters. That is, daughters are taught to cook, clean, mend clothes, and succeed outside the home, while boys are not; some African American mothers have 40-year-old "boys" living at home. We become overachievers and they become nonachievers--essentially becoming angry, irresponsible, indecisive, and noncommittal.

Second, in the workplace, where many African American men will say black women are taking jobs from Black men--or the "TWOFER" syndrome (that is, according to Affirmative Action rules, being Black and a woman counts twice as much, hence we are more likely hired). African American women, in turn feel betrayed and disappointed in them, and their continuing irresponsible behavior. In *The Piano Lesson*, a play by August Wilson, the aftermath of the brother/sister struggle is evident. The female character, Bernice, is trying to hold on to the family piano that to her represents where her family has come from slavery and consequent hard times. Boy Willie, her brother, looks to the future and wants to sell the piano so he might buy some land in the South. In short, their disagreement, and the following letters, represent the problems that we develop in "brotherly" relationships, those that frequently begin at home and are (we are super caretakers of all men) manifested in the workplace.

> " ...my relationship with my brothers is almost nonexistent. Boys will be boys. My two older brothers are nine and six years older than I. By the time I came along, my parents didn't want anything to do with a little girl. I do have a brother who is three years older than I. He and I used to be really close, until one day, I invited my boyfriend, who nobody liked, over while my parents were out of town. We were in my bedroom, another no-no, necking; and my

brother came home. He called me out of my room and told me that this guy had to go home. Once my boyfriend left, he attacked me and tried (no exaggeration) to strangle me...(there were certain roles that women took and men assumed in my parents eyes. They were determined to make me as independent as I could possibly be. Even as a teenager, my father stressed that I would not NEED a man. He wanted me and my sister to be able to fend for ourselves.) The irony of it is that my sister and I are the only two children, out of four boys and two girls, that have college degrees; and my sister is pursuing a graduate degree. I plan on it in the near future...it's funny they all said, 'you know how Stevie is'. Excuse me, I know how I am too and I don't think that the victim has to do the fence mending nor did I do anything that warranted strangulation..."

Kimberly, 22, single,
student, Minneapolis

" ...I was never close to my mother. However, I do remember that she was always making a fuss over my brother; e.g., no one in my family except my grandmother was allowed to punish or spank him, though it was not the same for me. I believe my mother loved me, she just preferred my brother, maybe because he was the youngest...now my brother and I still have a loving relationship, we have always held tight to each other especially since our mother died...but I do feel that I have provided the 'mother' figure for my brother. (My sister and I are 25 years apart and I also provided a maternal figure for her.) He never seemed to mature in many ways. He has lived a life in and out of various juvenile and prison institutions since the age of 11..."

Elisha, 42, separated, unemployed,
three sons, Baltimore

" ...in one word terrible. We have always been at odds with each other. I guess I was jealous of the attention my folks gave him when we were growing up. He is the athlete of the family and a lot of attention was given to him, I resented it and I guess I still do. Although my folks tried to explain to me I was the one they were least worried about, because they felt I could take care of myself. As an adult, my brother blamed the world for his less than perfect life-style...I work with several 'brothers' all of whom I have problems with. They put me down and make me feel guilty for being successful..."

Emma, 41, accountant,
mother of a five year old male child, Detroit

Kimberly and Elisha define the problem well. Kimberly said, "Boys will be Boys..." We've all heard that phrase. It's interpretation? They are not responsible for their behavior. Kimberly further supports that in her final statement, "You know how Stevie is." It also seems implicit that "Stevie" was a surrogate father--and like her real father wanted to run her life--not acceptable. Luckily Kimberly realized that her needs are just as, if not more, important than her brothers--regardless of what her family says. The other important point in Kimberly's letter is how she and her sister are in the process of overachieving--perhaps hoping that their parents will notice them (even telling her she wouldn't need a man). It seems her family unit values boys over girls. She probably can do everything from running a household to running a boardroom.

In Elisha's case that was stated plain and simple. "...I remember she was always making a fuss over my brother...I believe my mother loved me--she just preferred my brother..." It sounds as if she has "resolved" these issues because they now have a loving relationship since their mother died.

It may be because she is now the maternal figure and looks at her brother as her mother did--unable to take responsibility for his actions. " ...he has lived his life in and out of various juvenile and prison institutions..." Too bad for him, she is not responsible.

Emma has an almost identical problem, "I was jealous of the attention my folks gave him when we were growing up...my folks felt I could take care of myself...my brother blames the world for his less than perfect life-style...I work with several brothers...all of whom I have problems with...they make me feel guilty for being successful..." Though Emma has fallen prey to the guilt that African American brothers have made us feel.

She should not feel that being successful is synonymous with them being unsuccessful, nor do we take jobs away from our African American brothers or advance any quicker in the workplace. According to the AMERICAN ASSOCIATION FOR AFFIRMATIVE ACTION (see "Resources") Black women are still at the bottom of the economic, social, and political barrel. We continue to achieve because we have had to take care of ourselves and our children.

In fact, most of us are locked into low paying, low status jobs. We still earn an average salary of $13,000 to White women's $14,627. Our unemployment rate is still high at almost 15% this of course is complicated by the fact that more than 50% of our households are headed by Black women. The "TWOFER" syndrome does not apply.

A contributor says,

" ...I was raised in a matriarchal society, where my mom was head of the household due to an absentee father, as was my grandmother, aunt, and cousin. As a result, I have been taught to be totally self-sufficient..."

Lanette, 27, secretary, single,
one child, Ralrialto, CA

Lanette and I have learned that in our family units we were both socialized to "LEARN TO TAKE CARE OF YOURSELF" because a man won't be around long enough to be of use. (Clearly different from White women who are socialized to "marry up." We have to marry anybody and no, they frequently won't be around.)

Lanette really drives the point home. "I was raised in a matriarchal society due to an absentee father...I have been taught to be self-sufficient..." In my family unit the situation is identical. I have an underachieving 28-year-old brother still living at home rent and responsibility free, which frequently makes me angry. Lanette and I get tired of always being so responsible, such overachievers in comparison with boys, just like Wyomia. We need to learn to compete with ourselves only. That is, we should expect the best from ourselves. Difficult if we witness this complication.

" ...it was a long time before I understood that it was 'normal' for brothers and sisters to fight as they grew up. We fought a lot. We also spent a lot of time together, alone. We have always been real close. We were the only two children living with our parents for 12 years. At times, we felt like all we could depend on was each other. Yes, I guess there is some tension between us due to our parents' favoritism. We could feel it. My father's anger was projected onto my brother as we grew older. Also the older we became the more I became, my father's favorite; thus, the tension. My brother is a bit lighter (his skin) than I, and it seems my dark skin was a problem for him. He still calls me 'blackie' from time to time. He always called me that as we were growing up. I never liked it..."

Deidra, 50, divorced,
physician, New York City

" ...I had always wanted my 43-year-old brother to grow up and stop gaming; gaming me, and everybody, mostly I wanted him to stop dating White women. I thought if I introduced him to the right woman this would stop. I have introduced him to the 'right' woman, but he still can't make a commitment to anyone from making a phone call saying he won't be at work today or setting a date to see her. My husband says that he doesn't deserve the title of man..."

Minerva, 40, married, fashion consultant, Phoenix

Besides being responsible and overachieving to get attention (e.g., doing everything perfectly), we have to fight White women as well. The Black/White syndrome is played out full scale. If your brother chooses lighter-skinned or White women, you are already competing with him for attention, you begin to overachieve even more to get your parents' attention. (We may even fuel the fire with our lighter-skinned sisters.) We then begin to believe that no matter how wonderful we are, no one will ever notice us. Our self-esteem decreases (also see chapter six) a losing battle ensues.

Most important here is that our society, even in the African American community, has been socialized to covet White skin and blonde hair. As Spike Lee points out in his movie "Jungle Fever," and as one of my friends even went so far as to say, all Black men want White women (I call it the "ARLENE SYNDROME" --they all seem to be named or look like that). There are even some Black women who say that the White women that Black men choose are nonassertive, and will take abuse that Black women won't take. Some particularly angry Black women will also say that these White women are women White men don't want, are unattractive and not so smart. (These same Black women also believe conversely that some Black women who end up with White men are smart, attractive, assertive and have given up on Black men. Seldom, will you see an affluent White man with a low income Black woman.) The point is, most Black women's anger is directed at the shrinking pool of Black men, and rightfully so (71% of these relationships are Black men with White women). Worse, we spend a lot of time trying to straighten them and this problem out, as does Minerva.

We can not continue to compare ourselves to White anything regardless of what our men say or do; we may need to learn to love them less.

Deidra, despite her success, is still fighting with her "brother" and feeling bad about it. In fact, she is probably still comparing herself to what her brother thinks.

Minerva is very angry at her brother because she wants him to shape up, be responsible, make a commitment, and be decisive (date Black women). The only person who can make him grow up is himself (historically Black men have believed White women elevate them socially--that's not our problem). Minerva needs to redirect her efforts to her own life. He is responsible for himself--and probably suffers from low self-esteem. Both Deidra and Minerva need to love themselves more and him less.

As does this contributor:

> " ...my relationship with my two brothers has always been one of support. Although they are both older than I, I've always supported them. Whether it be with money, the use of my apartment, my car, or my love. They are takers and I am a giver. Even when we were children and had equal portions of things, whenever they would use theirs up, I gave them some of mine. I love them but at times it is difficult for me to respect them. They are just the opposite of me, very dependent where I am independent. We get along very well because they live in different states now; we would get along a lot worse if they lived here..."
>
> *Anonymous*

Wrong, wrong, wrong! If the scenario were rewritten Deidra, Minerva, and "Anonymous" would learn to love their brothers less, that is helping our brothers frequently means not helping them--but loving ourselves more. Even though "Anonymous'" parents raised them equally as children it appears that she has reinforced them for not giving her things she needed--such as love and support. All of these women must "unlearn" the game Wyomia was taught, which we can do!

THE 1-2-3 OF IT

We need to:

1. Not fall prey to our African American "brothers" making us feel guilty for achieving particularly in the work place. We are not "TWOFERs."

2. Not become overachievers and learn to compete with ourselves, not with our"brothers."

3. Learn that helping our "brothers" frequently means not helping them--loving them less and ourselves more. Allow them to be responsible for themselves. And remember, if they do not take up that responsibility, we are not to blame.

CHAPTER 5

Friends:
How can I Develop Good Friendships?

> "Friends won't let you down, friends will be around when you need them most of all, your friends...friends are hard to find, friends are yours and mine, you need them most of all your friends..."
>
> *Jody Watley, singer.*

Jody Watley and others have spoken of the true nature of friends. They are with us early in childhood as playmates to later in life as soul mates. However, many times what happens to us instead is we develop faulty, energy-draining relationships with people who are adding nothing to our lives.

This problem originates because many African-American women have difficulty accepting others doing things for them--particularly because we do, do, do for other people, everyone, in fact, except ourselves. When someone wants to "befriend" us we have a difficult time because we believe they want to "use" us as perhaps others have. Our needs are clearly not met in these types of relationships. We don't "befriend ourselves." We need to believe that friendships are a two-way street: you have to be receiving something to give something--giving all the time is not healthy. We need to reserve a little time for ourselves first. That might include developing a life on our own without these "so-called" friends and learning to be comfortable doing some things alone. Develop interests, not hobbies. As I think of my own friends, the development of sister/friendhood is clearly more special in the black community. This chapter speaks of the variability of these "friendships" from "acquaintances" to "sisters," "male friends," and "spiritual friends." These are the ones we want to learn to cherish.

> "...Mireya is the one friend out of the four that I see at least twice a month at the mall downtown. I have been meeting Mireya at the mall for about ten years. I consider my meetings with her therapeutic. She talks about her career and male relationships she has been involved in over the past years. I talk about my potential male relationships and my still aspiring career goals (smile). Mireya is my only lady friend that I borrow money from when my budget gets extremely tight. I remember one time when we met at the mall, after she came back from a very elaborate vacation abroad. My first response was, 'Welcome back to the poor side of town.' She asked what I meant by that statement. I said, 'Loan me $20'..."
>
> *Barbara, 36, single,*
> *telephone operator, New York City*

"...I do not have many friends. I am pretty much a loner, and only sometimes I enjoy it. I have problems with doing things on my own. I have one friend that I stay in touch with via the telephone; and I have met friends (associates) through work, but these have been mostly superficial and again facilitated via the telephone. I would like to have a close friend, but I feel such a friendship is usually made and cemented during childhood or even high school or college..."

Terry, 25, receptionist, Gainesville

Finding friends, any friend, seems particularly difficult for African American women as noted in comparing these two letters. Barbara has been fortunate in that she has developed such a relationship and has someone to lean on--asking for money has always been difficult for us. **(Remember we don't want anyone in our business.)**

Terry, on the other hand, is having this problem because she believes she missed out on her "window of opportunity" to develop a life-long friend. While childhood and college mark transitional times in which we usually develop such friendships, it is not impossible to maintain positive unions at any time. Terry needs to learn to befriend herself first and trust that she is "friendly," which will help her develop relationships like those discussed in the following group of letters:

"...I have been waiting for this part!! This could take ten pages. However, I'll only tell you about a few. Cissy is who can be considered my best friend. We met in high school and became friends when we both joined the track team. Actually I joined, she was the star and ended up getting an athletic scholarship to the University of Pittsburgh in 1978. I graduated high school in 1979. I had been accepted to Spelman but would have had to sit out one semester, because I applied late. I had also wanted to attend Emory University in Atlanta, never dreamed I wouldn't be accepted (I had a 3.8 on a 4.0 scale). Therefore, I didn't apply anywhere else. I was not accepted to Emory because my SAT scores were low. I was crushed. That is when I applied to Spelman (in May). A semester seemed like forever. Two weeks before classes were to begin at the University of Pittsburgh, the dean of the College of Arts and Sciences called me. His wife had been my advanced placement English teacher my senior year and was upset that I would be sitting out a semester. Anyway, two weeks later, I was a freshman at the University of Pittsburgh.

This may seem totally unrelated to Cissy's story, but years later I realized that it was all fate with no planning on our part. I ended up living next door to her in the dorm. That is when we became 'best friends.' Cissy lives in Philadelphia now. We haven't lived in the same city since she left Pittsburgh (a year before I did). There is nothing especially unique about our relationship except she is my best friend and not yours and not anyone else's...for example, I never give my books away. I may buy a person a copy of a book or photocopy a section, but I don't 'give my books.' Last month, I sent Cissy my copy of Itabari S. Njeri. It wasn't because I couldn't afford to buy her one. I wanted her to have the one I read. This woman's life (Itabari) sounds so much like Cissy's and mine, that I just wanted her to read the same book I read. I can't explain it any better than that. As I wrapped the book to be mailed I remember thinking, 'I must really love this girl to be giving her my book.' And I do..."

Shannon, 26, single,
college administrator, Atlanta

"...Barbara is my best friend. I do all of the listening. Sometimes I demand that she hear me out. As an eighth grader, I considered myself a seasoned writer and Barb was my only reader. I remember writing some of the sexiest love stories ever penned, and Barb enjoyed reading them and bugging me for the next story. She tells me today that there is a novel in me. I told her that I can't write a story I am still living. Barb is a good friend, my "bestest" friend, and I trust her completely. Barb tells me everything because she has a better memory for details. The only time I feel like an older sister to Barb is when it comes down to sex. She'd never forgive me for revealing the fact that she remained a virgin until age 29. We discussed what it would be like before it happened for her--long distance--I hope the operator wasn't listening (smile). The only sad part about it was that the guy didn't even know she was a virgin..."

Anonymous

"...Carol and I have been friends for about three years now. It seems, at a glance, that we have very little in common, except being female and African American. She is the mother of three children all over 21 years old, and I have none. She didn't finish high school; I went to college and am always taking courses somewhere. She would like not much more than a man to take care of her. The thought of someone 'taking care of me' or worse, a man taking care of me scares the shit out of me. The list goes on. Yet, it seems as though we have the same soul--kindred spirits in some sense. She knows more about me; I have told her more than anybody. Of all my friends, I trust her most. It isn't that I distrust my other close friends, I just wouldn't hesitate telling Carol anything..."

Terry Lynn, 32, single,
administrative assistant, Ann Arbor

All of these women point out the unique specialness of our friendships, it may be that we share a secret as in "Anonymous" of her friend's virginity or something even more basic such as sharing a book (as in Shannon's case) or the ability to talk about anything (as in Terry Lynn's case). These letters outline the "special bond" we have with our best friends. We will, and typically do, do anything for these women, and what's best is that they frequently last longer than the men in our lives.

Selena, my long time friend of 20 plus years, has had the same effect on me. While seemingly we have very little in common (her cancer, my graduate school, the birth of her daughter Kendal, my up and down love life), we have managed to maintain the relationship we developed in childhood. What best binds us is "OURSTORY," we don't have to explain so many things: our hair, for example. One of my favorite organizations is GIRLFRIENDS (see Resources) which supports ongoing long-term relationships between women. They have a newsletter, Chatterbox, which promotes ongoing information between friends and associates. In Terry McMillan's book, *Disappearing Acts,* the friendship between Zora and her cast of friends well illustrates the potential relationship that exists between us, and is inherently there between all African Americans every time we speak to each other on the street. White people don't do that: acknowledge that it's rough out there, such as what is noted in the following letter:

> "...being in another country is so different. Exciting and stressful at the same time. Even here in Scotland you experience that you are an American. In the U.S., they do not like you because you are black. I feel I have it hard all the way around sometimes. So as a black female I find therapy in being with my other black female friends, so we get together and talk about anything..."
>
> *Juliette, 29, single, U.S. Navy,*
> *two children, son, age 8; daughter, 3*

The situation for Juliette is that race draws her sisters together. We can always "KITCHEN TABLE IT," even if we have little in common as Selena and I do. Many times we get involved in relationships with men which are not firmly grounded in friendship:

> "...Paul is a former lover of mine from the University here. Our relationship didn't end too well; and I never thought we would speak to each other, let alone be good friends. After five years of no contact, Paul called me because he heard that I was sick (his mother and I stay in touch). We have been talking ever since. Paul is a journalist in New

Jersey. It was writing that brought us together. No, actually, it was lust, which turned into the realization that we both loved to write...then we fell in love. Even though we stumbled through most of the relationship, it was one of the best relationships that I have ever had..."

Paulette, 45, engaged,
editor, New York City

Paulette makes a good point about our relationships with men. We don't develop underlying friendships before we fall into bed (see "Chapter Six"). It is the friendships that make long-term relationships with our men, as she found out much later. Besides "surrounding ourselves" with supportiveness, another way of befriending ourselves is spiritually, as these women say:

"...I know a lot of people who have many acquaintances. I certainly have those I can talk to, but to me, a friend is a very special person; and the only friend I have learned to love and trust is Jesus..."

Anonymous

"...I don't have very many people that I call friends, but for the few that I do have I am grateful to Allah for sending them...he is truly my friend..."

Sara, 35, divorced,
unemployed, Joliet

Both of these women outline the necessity of having a spiritual presence in our lives (more on that in "Chapter 11"). Some of us unfortunately feel like this--quite lost:

"...I have been in California for about nine years. I haven't really been in contact with any high school or early college friends. When I would return home for a vacation and look some of them up, I realized that our lives were very different. They were usually married with a couple of children, and I, on the other hand, was advancing at a great pace in my career...since I arrived, I found it difficult to make many real close friends. I am beginning to think that my standards are much too high, and that is why I don't have very many friends. I divide the ones I do have into three categories: the first are really true friends, the ones I would trust with my life, who are honest with me and I am honest with them, there is a great respect between us, and in this category I have zero friends. The second category are friends with whom I have conversations with about once a month, where we catch up on each others lives and say we will get together and don't. In this category I have about five friends. The last category is for the friends I have lost over the years since I have been in California and that number is about 20...I have tried to seek out positive, focused, and active individuals and found that people talk about these things all the time with little or no follow through. So we remain 'friends' until this point is made evident, then the lines of communication begin to shut down; and I find we didn't have that much in common after all..."

Anonymous, Oakland

How then does this contributor and our first contributor, Terry, find and keep good friends? First, besides befriending themselves, they must develop interests not hobbies. Interests are things that are part of our lives; activities that you can share with someone on an ongoing basis. Hobbies are things that you do to waste time. This squandering of time is most evident if we won't go to movies, concerts, or comparable activities alone. We feel unloved if our answering machine blinks "0" at us or, worse, if we are at home all day and the phone doesn't ring. We will, of course, drop everything if "our friend" wants us to go to the local "in spot," perhaps with the idea of picking up a man (friends first, remember!). We can only find a friend if we are good friends, that is, with something to offer-for instance, warmth, supportiveness, intimacy, and trust for starters. More than that, we need a life of our own and then interesting activities that can be shared will follow. Are there things that you've wanted to try and never did? Didn't want to do them alone? It is time to take the first step. I remember a client, a dance major, who badly wanted to see the Alvin Ailey Dance Company, but had never seen a live dance performance--too embarrassed, too shy, too afraid to be seen alone at this "type of function." i told her that she was only denying herself the experience of seeing Alvin Ailey, but 'responsible' for everyone else having a bad time, because everyone would be pointing at her because she was ALONE!

After she saw how she was shortchanging herself and those she could share this experience with, she changed her mind and went. Needless to say, she has now seen Alvin Ailey many times. We need to do things alone. We all should have a wealth of experiences we can bring to relationships. In any relationship we have to give to get something back--and if we don't have something to offer such as interests, who would want to have us as friends? Best of all, we will be the best friend any one person can have, they are the lucky ones to have us!

THE 1-2-3 OF IT

We need to:

1. Befriend ourselves first regardless--Spend time with people that include us in activities that we are interested in. We are more likely to find people who could be potential friends at activities that we enjoy. If basketball is an interest--go to games. If art is a fascination--go to openings. They are obviously interested in them as well, or they wouldn't be there.

2. Develop interests not hobbies--hobbies are fleeting time wasters that you use when bored--not really a part of your lifestyle. Interests are regularly incorporated into your personhood, as I noted above.

3. Attend an activity even if you will be alone. Some of my best fun was going alone and watching and meeting people and then going back to a discouraging "associate" telling them how much fun it was.--This gives a sense of accomplishment.

Our communication or lack thereof–not sex or money is our number one problem.

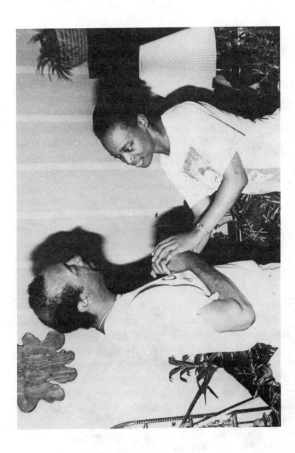

Relationships really are an evolutionary process: boyfriend, lover, husband and possibly parent.

Chapter 6

Boyfriends, Lovers, Husbands, and Kids: How We Get In and Out of Relationships!

"Relationships are the fabric of life..." Faith Ringold, quiltmaker-artist, and writer.

Actually Ms. Ringold didn't say those words, she would have, I'm sure, if given the opportunity. In my struggle to conceptualize this chapter (and my own relationships), I began reading her illustrated story also a quilt, Tar Beach, which describes the complex relationship between a man and a woman and the positive effect it has on their daughter. Another of her quilts, "church picnic story", illustrates a wonderful book, *Memory of Kin*, by Mary Helen Washington. This book also describes the delicate balance of our relationships and supports the idea that our primary relationships (mother, father, sister, and brother) do influence our secondary relationships (boyfriends, lovers, husbands, and kids).

Some African American women complain that Black men are indecisive, irresponsible, and can't make a commitment. Some Black men have countered that we are difficult and demanding. The best thing about these heated discussions, of course, is that we are talking to one another about what is clearly a problem. Our communication or lack thereof--not sex or money--is our number one problem. It is the getting in and getting out of these relationships that results in our most volatile feelings, ranging from passive constraint to active rage in our lives.

Relationships really are an evolutionary process: boyfriend, lover, husband (maybe even parent). When we decide to leave him, it is also a process: anxiety, anger, and assessment, more on that later. What we haven't learned is that a bad relationship is worse than no relationship, because we are still socialized subtly that men, even bad ones, make us whole people. We continue to be more passive at home than in the workplace. Consequently, we are so anxious to hook anyone, usually a bad someone, it results in choosing the wrong man again and again and again (see "Chapter 2"--CYCLE OF MEN). More specifically, it is this process that we must understand. I frequently emphasize the "friend" in boyfriend because, as with our girlfriends, these are people we can talk to about anything. That is what intimacy is: the ability to share feelings and develop trust. We rarely do this with men first, but that is the only way the relationship will last. What happens is we get these steps out of order, or forget about ourselves and our lives once we are in a relationship. As I said in the "Introduction," a relationship is a 100-100 thing not a 50-50 one. We need to get ourselves together, find someone who is together and then proceed. We can't make anyone change (e.g., better) in a relationship. We can only change ourselves for the better.

Note the following contribution:

"...I met my boyfriend when I was 15, a sophomore in high school. Even though I went to an all girls' high school, a friend of mine had shown my picture to this guy, and he told her he wanted to meet me. That was in 1971. Through my attending college in Ohio and his going into the Marines (he dropped out of college his freshman year; played too much instead of going to class), we maintained our relationship. He proposed to me at age 21. I wasn't ready. He proposed to me at 22. I still wasn't ready for marriage. I became pregnant at 23. When I went to him and told him he asked, 'What do you want me to do about it?' I told him I had to think about it. I did think about it. The only recourse I thought I had at the time was to have an abortion. He said that he couldn't give me any money toward it because he didn't have any. (I also have to mention here that I was in no better financial position than he was to have paid the $175 for the abortion.) I was working full time to try to finish my degree. Yes, had this not occurred at this time I would have my B.A. right now...I am still bitter about it, if he had just given me more emotional support, I probably would have gone on and finished my course that summer. But I was an emotional wreck, I could not...this from a man I had known for eight years. A man who acted as though I was everything in the world to him...I went through this experience all alone. All alone except for one girlfriend who came to pick me up and take me to have it done. She came to pick me up afterwards and spent the evening with me until I told her it was okay for her to go home...a white girlfriend I might add. She and I are still friends to this day...anyway, I went through a very hard time after this procedure. I am Catholic and aside from dealing with the whole thing, I was feeling very, very angry at this man who had helped me to conceive a child, but who could bear no responsibility for doing so. Even when I would start to cry and get upset he would just say to me, 'Why keep crying about it?: It is over now.' I still remember how I felt more vividly than I would like to...I still dated him, though I wouldn't allow myself to have sexual relations with him for two months. Even though I was still terrified that I would get pregnant again, even though precautions were being taken by both of us. Needless to say, at 25 I became pregnant again. The same thing happened all over, except this time, I went through the whole abortion all by myself. No girlfriends, because I had become more ambiguous about the whole abortion issue and felt friends I had would not understand. I also thought I could not tell my girlfriend who had been with me the first time because she would have a fit! She never would have understood how I would allow myself to become pregnant a second time by the same man. To tell the truth I can hardly believe it myself. I could see it if I were stupid or just plain dumb, but: I am not. I think of myself as a very intelligent and worldly woman. How could this happen again? Of course, the price had gone up to $225 this time, so again I had to use my finances to take care of the situation. I was again emotionally devastated. No one knew this time around except for he and I. I have carried this burden around with me for the last 11 years of my life. I would have two children by now, ten and eight years of age...it is very painful. I cannot honestly sit here and tell you that I was ready to become a mother either of those times, obviously I felt that I was not. That does not make the pain any less painful...the thing that bothers me now is that in 1983 I went to Alaska for a year, I felt I needed to get away from Kansas City. And, yes, from this man who seemed to have this hold over me. He called me faithfully the first five months I was there. We would talk, and he would ask me repeatedly when I was coming home. I kept telling him I didn't know. He said. 'Please come home I need you. I love you.' I still loved him, as I still do now to some extent. I didn't return home. He married this girl that he said he had just met. They were married in March of 1984 and divorced in November of 1985. He now has a five-year-old daughter that he values above any and everything. What is difficult for me is that he accepted this child with open and willing arms when he stood by and sanctioned the killing of the two children that we conceived together. I don't care that he was married and that his wife became pregnant. Is she any better a woman than I am that he should allow her child to live and mine to die? I feel very bitter about this...I have not seen him since May of this year. I told him that I wanted us to be friends. He did not want that. He wants more. He has asked me again to marry him. I cannot. I also don't think our goals and values are alike. I want a man who is financially stable, I don't think he is. I also need to interject here, while I was living in New York, he impregnated another woman who had a paternity suit filed against him. And he is not only paying child support for his own child by his ex-wife, he is also paying child support for this other woman's child. It is just all too much for me to take. I don't want to have to deal with all of this and I don't...the saddest thing about all of this is that I still love him..."

Anonymous, Kansas City

"Anonymous, Kansas City" has made the same mistake many of us have made, staying involved with the wrong man, which begins with not utilizing the "friend" part of boyfriend. As in Chapter Five, the development of positive relationships, even with a man, requires friendship first. We rarely make this mistake with female friends who do us wrong multiple times. How can we expect to develop long-term, intimate (e.g., sexual) involvement with someone who is not trustworthy or dependable--we all know sex-only relationships are very unfulfilling. We need to understand that all intimate relationships are process oriented--that is, they develop and change over time.

She drives the point home so much so that she knew that she was not ready for a committed relationship early on..."He proposed to me at 21. I wasn't ready. He proposed to me at 22. I wasn't ready..." to the ultimate mistake of getting pregnant at 23--clearly they were not ready to become responsible lovers. Unfortunately, when she became pregnant and decided alone to have an abortion "Anonymous" did not have a friend to help make that decision. As if that weren't enough, the same thing happened again! Unfortunately this young woman didn't feel comfortable enough to rely on her friend to get her through this ordeal. Also evident is that she does not know the value, importance or the "how to's" of friendship (see Chapter Five).

In fact when "Anonymous" does describe a friendship, she refers to"...a White girlfriend..." as though a White friend is the only one who can be counted on. Wrong! She simply needs to get back to basics on developing relationships. A friend could have helped her make a very difficult decision.

"...The only recourse I thought I had was to have an abortion..." The choice to terminate a pregnancy is a difficult one, making choices means getting all the information before you make the decision which she did not do. Besides dealing with the guilt many of us might feel, there are medical and psychological implications that need to be addressed. The NATIONAL ABORTION RIGHTS ACTION LEAGUE (NARAL) and, of course, PLANNED PARENTHOOD (see "Resources") could have provided information on her choices. YES, he needed to be involved more than financially. It is a difficult decision regardless of how many times you have to make it. Emotional support is crucial. "...why keep crying about it? It's over now..." He was not there for her as a friend should be. Ultimately what happens (and what's happening to "Kansas City") is that we forget this step, as I described in Chapter Two, the "CYCLE OF MEN." We get burned by a guy, leave, and return to the same guy hoping by some miracle that he has changed--wrong, he hasn't because he doesn't want

to. In fact, he has repeated this behavior with
women (except they made him accountable par[
filing paternity suits). He continues this "hold" o[
although she has left. The saddest line of the letter
to be "I...still love him..." I would like to underline [
that no one has a hold on us, we are totally respons[
for our own happiness.

African American women are often confused by the
definition of love. Love is not shown in this letter. In
fact, love is not painful, it contains no emotional manipula-
tion or physical abuse. It feels good. Like a quilt, you
feel safe and secure because this is based on trust and
mutual support that comes from friendship first--like
this woman has:

> "...I am seeing someone, and for the most part, I am very
> happy with him. He is my friend and that is the most
> important aspect of our relationship. He is kind, con-
> siderate, thoughtful, debonair, cool (extremely cool),
> sensitive and romantic. Our relationship is in the early
> stages yet, and we both agree to take it one day at a time.
> He loves me unlike any man ever has, I thank God for
> him. We are different emotionally. I tend to get very
> excited about things and am more outgoing; conversely,
> he is very private and shy. We both have our insecurities
> about the relationship and hate to fight because it feels
> so bad. Recently I told him that every couple has dis-
> agreements and that it is natural to fight, and healthy.
> At least we know what we want and don't want. We are
> sure that we want to be together, but our insecurities
> can get in the way and make things difficult. I hope we
> can make it..."

Lily, 35,
high school teacher, Indiana

Lily's boyfriend has all the earmarks of a potential
positive relationship. She describes her boyfriend as
a "...friend, supportive, kind, considerate..." Lily realized emotional and physical intimacy are one and the
same. She goes on to state their differences, how they
handle them and the developing intimacy; but best of
all how it happens over time--not in a couple of
days--and it all leads to the next stage of a relation-
ship--lovers.

LOVERS

Becoming lovers is a big step. It may mean commitment
or perhaps just a deepening of the relationship, but
mostly it means change or another level of intimacy
to which the following women all will attest:

"...tonight I tried to suppress the desire to call my man. I realize that if he has not called by this time to arrange to see me, he must be involved in one of his projects that often take up a lot of his time. I finally gave in to the desire and dialed his phone number. After some small talk, I heard him uncomfortably trying to explain why he had not been in touch. He apologized, and stated that he had not intended to neglect me, but family commitments and his devotion to his current art project had been in the forefront this particular week. As we hung up, I felt sad. Sad first for my apparent neediness and sad next that it took these types of conservations in order for him to see that perhaps he should be more attentive to our relationship. I do not deny the fact that I am angry, angry about my seeming dependency on this man. It occurred to me that I need him much more than he needs me. I must let go of these dependent feelings and regain my strength. I cannot help but wonder: in doing so will I lose my man?..."

Anonymous, Kentucky

"...I have been dating one man for six months. He is three years younger than I and not on the same educational level. I now know that nice is much better than money. He is in the process of completing his degree and is very ambitious. He is quite supportive of me in my struggles in the corporation which seems to be a rarity in black men, particularly those who are doctors and lawyers (I have dated my share)..."

Theda, 30, single, attorney with the JC Penny Corporation, Texas

"...I'm not really looking for a man to marry. I have long ago given up on that. But I would like a relationship/friendship and I can understand why more and more black women are slowly giving up on black men as potential mates and turning to other races for companionship and affection. It seems as if there is always something, some hinderance sabotaging the potential committed relationship between black men and women. Black men seem to have a difficult time opening up and then it means that the female has to be the male and the female in the relationship. I think it is unfair for us to have to take the man's role in a mature male/female relationship. White men, or those I've taken as lovers, don't seem to have that problem..."

Anonymous, Philadelphia

"...I have two lovers one is six years older than I and the other is two years older than I. Both are included in my list of five best friends. Both know that I see someone else, and we all accept and respect the honesty and give each other the freedom to see other people. Neither feel insecure in our relationship because of the open communication, respect and honesty that we share. I enjoy the best of both worlds because I am able to experience different things with each one. They are similar in many ways but very different in others. I love them both. I couldn't ask for better lovers and/or friends..."

Sheryl, 25, single, administrator
human resources, San Francisco

"...the relationship with McKinley and I was once perfect until distance got in the way. He and I met in a training program. We spent nine months together. Before graduation, we decided that our feelings were stronger than we had expected. The only problem we had was that I was going to Michigan and he was going to Alabama. Despite the distance, our relationship is wonderful. I know he loves me. We talk on the phone about everything, and even though we meet from time to time in Kentucky, Michigan, and Chicago we have only made love once. He is the kind of guy who falls in love first and then takes it from there. The only problem that we have is that we sometimes hold back our true feelings. This has a lot to do with us not seeing each other on a day-to-day basis. So when we do get together everything is perfect and why wouldn't it be. We are now debating on whether or not just to end it or have one of us move. This has not been easy for me. We know that we don't have much to base this decision on, only love and sometimes that just isn't enough..."

Anonymous, Michigan

All of these women have different intimate relationships with the lovers in their lives. The first letter highlights a common problem in our relationships, "ONESIDEDNESS" with African American men. While in many relationships, couples go through give and take, clearly our first contributor is the more "needy" in her relationship. It sounds as if she does all of the initiating, planning of activities, etc. She also is probably always there for him. No doubt she believes that if she is there for him, he will come to his senses and be there for her. Of course, that has never materialized. Unfortunately it doesn't work quite that way. That is, we need to know relationships require both parties to give 100 percent; it's not a 50-50 thing. This is a very hard lesson to learn but, we as African American women need to learn that we have loved too much and gotten too little in return. Not acceptable.

Theda and "Anonymous, Philadelphia" point out the problems that Black women have finding lovers or potential committed relationships with Black men. Theda talks about dating out of her "social/work class" and discovering, as many of us need to, that there are available Black men willing to make a commitment that may not be "high power corporate types." The difficulties that these women experience are related to power. The balance of power in our relationships with our men is significant. Ask any professional woman who is also in a "financial" relationship with her man in which she makes more money and she will say, "I can't understand why this is an issue for him, I am extremely down to earth." "I can't find a man who isn't threatened by me or my position." We as Black women have forgotten that work is frequently most important to our men, and if we are doing better at "work" then we can probably do without them. Men read that and are hesitant to be involved with a "professional woman." The easiest solution to this is simple communication (well perhaps not so simple), but we certainly need to look at all the possibilities of available Black men. We need to talk it out.

"Anonymous Philadelphia" has taken the route that many African American women have, which is to give up on Black men altogether--I don't believe that is the real answer. While I certainly support anyone's choice to choose a White man, I still believe that African American men are the best on earth and with our support, they can be great mates. Condemning them only increases the pot of men who have given up on themselves.

Sheryl and "Anonymous, Michigan" both demonstrate that we are capable of having healthy relationships with lovers. While both of these women are at either end of the spectrum (I'm sure Sheryl is practicing safe sex, loving in a noncommitted way does work for her), both show the rockiness and process of making a commitment. Most important, both parties are whole individuals willing to make a choice to be with one another. There are no guarantees, even in marriage.

MARRIAGE

The big M, ultimate commitment--and certainly not a step to be taken lightly. African American women, however, have been socialized to believe that without a MRS. we are not whole, complete, and certainly not women. That is why many times if we do make the ultimate commitment to men who will not do right by us, we will stay anyway for the sake of the family, community, our parents, whatever, all clearly to our detriment. We need to find marital partners who are willing to make the same kind of commitment as we are to this life choice, as all of these women are struggling with:

> "...I think that this is my time to find out who I am and what my needs are. My husband and I are currently separated and have been for over four years. We split for various reasons, the primary being he began smoking crack

cocaine and I was not aware (or I didn't want to accept the knowledge). He was never a very emotional person and very noncommittal. We married when I was 17 years old and he was 25. He never remembered birthdays, anniversaries, Christmas, or any other holidays. He is very selfish with his money, and he didn't want to pay the rent, etc. I was married before I was old enough to learn how to pick a spouse and see that I had a lot of growing to do before being ready to commit. We rarely talk. He is currently living with a woman and doing the same things to her that he did to me...the only thing that I miss is the fun times and the person he was prior to the drug addiction..."

Anonymous, Daly City, California

"...my husband and I had a very good relationship for the first two years of our marriage. However, we have been married now for three-and-a-half years and the past 18 months have been difficult and painful. We have reached a point in our relationship where there is no communication. I am not quite sure how, when, or why we arrived at this stage, but it is quite painful. He stopped telling me important things, and he stopped inviting me out. The only thing we seem to share is sex. This is quite disturbing to me because I can't perform sexually since I have been trying to figure out what is going on with my marriage. I have been trying desperately to communicate with my husband, and all he will say is, "I don't want to talk. Everything is fine." We have been getting into heated arguments, and he says nasty things to me. After each argument he expects me to forget the entire argument and just move on as though nothing has happened. I can't understand why someone that I love and someone who claims to love me could treat me in such cruel ways. He is never around when I need him, and to him it is no big deal. The night before I had a major exam he went out with some of his friends, and he did not come home until 7:00 a.m., when I was on my way out of the door. He did leave a note on the kitchen table saying that he hoped I did well on my test. When he got home and I told him how disappointed I was that he chose to stay out all night and didn't call. He told me it was, "No big deal." He couldn't understand why I was making a fuss because he was sure there were thousands of people taking the exam without someone to be home for them. He says that it is always my fault...I feel like I am about to explode. I feel like I am really coming apart, like I am losing a part of my soul...I remember my vows but this is not the worst that I had contemplated. I believed worse was unemployment, underemployed, family illnesses, failure in school, not lack of communication and mental abuse. I believe communication and honesty are the bases for any good relationship. I do know when it is time to leave a marriage.

I believe it is time to leave when you can no longer cope, when you can no longer function as a unit, when you are losing your dignity and self-respect, when you are basically falling apart..."

Anonymous, Bronx

"...I married the father of my daughter, even though she was three at the time; mostly because I want my child to have a father. I really thought that I was in love. For nine-and-a-half years, I tried to have the family I never had as a child, but my husband was very abusive, physically and emotionally...the problem is I can't figure out if I am in love with him or in love with love because I so much want a family. Most important, I want to be the most important person in the life of the man that loves me. People always say that when it happens you will know. All I know is there are times when I want nothing more than to be his wife, and then there are times when all I want is to be by myself because there is uncertainty on my behalf about him. I know if I can't find happiness within myself, certainly no one else can provide happiness for me..."

Anonymous, Virginia

"...the relationship with my husband is very good. He is also my best friend...in fact, I consider him my soul mate. We have struggled and accomplished together and have excellent debates. We have been together for 14 years; married for 11 years and dated three years before that. The fact that we can't have children pretty much pulled us even closer together...naturally there is the hunger for the kind of passion that was present when we first met, but most of the time it is so much better than that..."

Phyllis, 46, married,
family relations counselor, New Haven

"...I am involved in a long-distance relationship that has lasted six years. We are getting married in October of this year. I have been divorced ten years; he has been a widower for 25 years. He is nine years older than I, and he is the first man I have known intimately that is significantly older. I care for him a great deal, not passionately but affectionately. He is kind, gentle, and caring. Our upbringings were similar and we have what I feel is important for successful male/female relationships. Although I feel we are both ready to make major changes in our lives we are both a little apprehensive. For my part, I have enjoyed my time on my own; and I hope I have learned to carve out time for myself so that my personal space will be maintained. For his part, he has been on his own unencumbered twice as long as I, without the burden of family accountability. I worry about both of our abilities to adjust to being a "twosome" once again, but I am confident that our love and knowledge will assist us in dealing with the rough spots..."

*Madeline, 51, single (soon to be married),
bank operations officer, Madison*

"...my husband and I have been married for 21 years, that in itself is pretty heavy duty. We have both changed over time, luckily we have grown closer together rather than apart. I have learned many things about marriage that I would like to share with you: we cannot make people be the people we want them to be. We are dependent yet separate. We want to control the people we love at one time or another. There are no guarantees in a relationship. Sometimes our best is not good enough and that is okay. We are our own worst enemy and critic. It is possible to love more than one significant other at the same time, but one should never jeopardize the primary relationship for the 'thrill of it all'. It is easier to ask for forgiveness than permission. You must respect yourself before you can demand respect from others. Marriage is a full-time job. It is hard to trust another person. Nothing is gained if risks are not taken. When you love someone you want to know everything about them..."

*Alice, 42, married,
homemaker, Lansing*

Different types of marriages all meeting a variety of needs some healthy, some unhealthy. All of the positive relationships (the latter letters) clearly began with friendship. Remember the lesson at the beginning of the chapter! Phyllis, Madeline, and Alice all note the importance of independence, communication, and knowing you and your partners likenesses and differences and the ways in which you can overcome the differences. Alice even provides us with a set of rules that have made her marriage successful. All of them also make the point that they were mature when they made the decision to commit to marriage which our first contributor, "Anonymous, Daly City, California," was missing. "...I think it is time to find out who I am and what my needs are...we married when I was 17..."

Most of the time, marrying at a young age is suicide. Our twenties, for example, is such a period of growth and change we can't possibly make a real commitment to anyone as "Anonymous, Daly City, California" found out. Now she is getting the chance to do some much needed growing. In her case, separation does not necessarily mean divorce. It can be a healthy way for both partners to do some work on themselves. If they decide to reconcile, they will come back as different people; and it will be a different relationship, hopefully for the better. She needs a partner who is drug free, who is going to communicate, and who will make an emotional and financial commitment; however, what she needs now is to take care of herself not him, which she has been doing for too long.

The communication problems that are evident in "Anonymous Bronx" are very common in Black couples. (If they are not talking to you before marriage, unless he decides to do some growing, he is not going to do it afterward either.) "...I've been trying to communicate with my husband, but all he will say is I don't want to...I believe communication and honesty are the bases of a good relationship..." Communication is the basis for any relationship--worse here because he won't communicate his needs to her and she keeps trying to figure them out. Impossible! We can't figure what other people need, and she should stop trying. Her sexual "difficulties" as well are related to this. Sex is another form of communication. As a result, she has noticed increased arguing for them and decreased self-esteem for her. The relationship then begins to topple like a "house of cards." It is time for her to separate, because her needs are not being met, and she must make herself whole again. (She clearly can't help him--he needs to do it himself.) Emotional abuse is not acceptable and it is a good reason to leave a relationship. As she said "...I believe it is time to leave when you can no longer cope...when you are losing your dignity and self-respect ...leave..." She's right, it's time.

"...I married the father of my baby, even though she was three at the time, mostly because I wanted my child to have a father..." Probably the worst reason to get married love based on a fairy tale. (Actually, one of the funniest letters I got was from a woman who had decided her Prince Charming may never come so she had decided to proceed with her life without him.) Many of us believe in "happily ever after"--even though we have every reason in the world not to. I think "Anonymous, Virginia," points out the problem well in that we frequently fall in love with the idea of love not love itself. Someone who is emotionally and physically abusive is not in your best interest. You may love him during the few periods he is nice to you, but it is probably not consistent enough to warrant riding out the storm. Love is not painful. Fortunately, she has realized that..."I know that if I can't find happiness

withinmyselfcertainlynooneelsecanprovidehappiness..."
She, "Anonymous, Daly City, California," and "Anonymous, Bronx" have all made the same error. We can only change ourselves not other people. He has to be willing to make necessary changes--and we need to do the same. If he can't, leaving is necessary.

Leaving a relationship is no easy feat either, there are stages, just as relationships didn't begin over night they don't end over night. It is a process and a painful one at that.

It begins with ANGST. Here is when we feel as one would describe "OUT OF CONTROL!" This is the first stage of ending a relationship in which we want to leave and stay. We feel we will lose what we have had (even though it no longer exists) and feel afraid this is the only man for us--if only he would change things it would be perfect, like a fairy tale. (Fannie, a writer friend of mine describes it as desperate love; she's right, you are desperate.) ANGER is the next stage, we get angry in a relationship if there is evidence of infidelity, problems with money, or if lack of communication is the culprit; and because we are so reticent to express these feelings, it makes us feel guilty and we are no longer nice. At the end of a relationship, we usually explode--perhaps even after a small occurrence--and pack our bags without expressing those feelings or we over express those feelings (such as to cause physical harm to our partners). Thus, carrying baggage to our next encounter.

The last stage ASSESSMENT is the stage we almost always forget. We frequently go from angst to anger with each man that we have a relationship with. The assessment stage is very important and this is where we actually assess what went wrong and come to terms with it. If we don't go through this stage we will repeat the same mistakes over and over and over (similar to the "CYCLE OF MEN"). Worse is when these unresolved feelings adversely affect other relationships, such as with our kids.

KIDS

Entire books have been written about rearing our children (many published by African American Images). Two good ones are: *Developing Positive Self-Images* and *Discipline in Black Children* and *The Conspiracy to Destroy Black Boys: Vols. I, II,* and *III* by Dr. Jawanza Kunjufu. What is consistent in most of the literature regarding rearing children is 1) our parenting has taken a variety of forms as the following contributors outline, 2) our declining lack of involvement with the extended family and community, and 3) the inability or lack of interest in taking care of ourselves first.

"...I have had zero children by birth; 27 by choice...I have a warm relationship with nieces, nephews, godchildren..."
Margaret, single, 48, artist, New Mexico

"...I am divorced. I have two daughters, a son, and a grandson of whom I have legal custody. For a while things were pretty hectic between my oldest and myself. She was always a taker and not a giver. However, over the past two to four years we have begun to heal the wounds of being a dysfunctional family. I have continued to be honest with her, which keeps the trust factor in the forefront for me. She has given me the reward of realizing I was in her corner, even though she didn't always feel that way. We are slowly becoming friends and having the kind of relationship that I want with her. My youngest daughter is the total opposite of my first daughter. We have always been friends. We have not always agreed, but the love always has been there between us. She has been there for me with the understanding of a child watching her mother trying to survive. She is very mature for her 14 years. We work on our problems together as much as possible. My son was a concern to me in that I thought I had raised a whiny, clinging, scared little boy. However, in the past eight months he has changed tremendously. He has become more confident and independent. He is more outgoing and stands up for himself. I still worry about his lack of some male contact, which I feel is important to all boys, but seems to be managing pretty well. My grandson is a very big concern to me because he was born angry and still is. I am having a hard time trying to pinpoint how to handle this problem. I have noticed that he responds better to situations where I am able to give him that 'extra attention.' My biggest problem is being able to know when he is in need of that attention and how much he needs, because he is so angry. He has come a long way from the screeching, crying two-year-old who constantly rebelled and broke things and threw tantrums to a five-year-old who talks about his feelings and knows that there are choices and consequences--good or bad--for his actions. The real change in my children has been me. The more I change my ways of doing things the more they change. I have learned that children react to the conditions and attitudes of the parents. I must be doing something right. My oldest graduated from high school at 16. Both my son and daughter have been on the honor roll all year and my grandson is now doing quite well in kindergarten..."
Sharazad, 42, divorced, unemployed, Philadelphia

"...my husband and I have two wonderful children: 15 and 10 years old. My daughter is the older of the two. We have a very good relationship. I encourage her to join and attend any and all school functions. We talk about anything and everything. We laugh together and cry together. She is a member of the honor society, the track team, the cross-country team, student council, the local 4-H Club, and a starting player on the high school basketball team. I attend everything with her. My son is just beginning to become involved in school activities. He does play baseball and he also attends his sister's activities with us. He doesn't mind because he says that is time is next and he knows I will go with him to everything. I help my children learn about all sports and activities in which they participate. I play basketball with them. I play softball, baseball, and tennis with them...I know that my children are a gift and I cherish that gift and will take care of them..."

Anonymous, Detroit

"...I am a single parent by choice. My daughter, age ten, and I have a healthy relationship; however, I think that she is too attached to me. I am allowing her attachment to keep me from developing friendships and meaningful relationships with other people. My child seems to get jealous when anyone shows an interest in me or when anyone (especially men and small children) seem attracted to me. My child and I have more of a friendship than a typical mother/daughter relationship. We participate in many activities together such as attending concerts, going to movies, shopping, and listening to music. She is very mature for her age and has an intelligent sense of humor. We have fun together, every night it is like a slumber party. Perhaps I am trying to develop a friendship with her that I did not have with other girls in my childhood. Nevertheless, I am afraid that my daughter will be emotionally devastated if something should happen to me. On the other hand, she is a good child, obedient and well disciplined. Yet, her attachment for physical affection concerns me. She does not understand my need for companionship with other people, particularly my need for intimacy..."

Meryl, single, 40, engineer, Louisville

"...my son (age 23) and daughter (age 28) are both professionals and share an emotional renaissance with me. Our relationship has evolved from my nurturing side of parenting to the supportive, adult challenge which presents itself daily. We are finding strength together in our individual ways of living in and responding to a racist society. My daughter and I are also struggling with sexism in corporate and public sector America. My son's needs as a black-corporate male differ from ours, yetweareabletosharevision,triumph,anddisappointments and most of all humor over the varying degrees to which societal issues affect us..."

Marianne, 49, divorced, administrator
Commonwealth of Massachusetts, Boston

Extended parenting, single parenting, traditional parenting--all of these letters point out the problems in parenting, and solutions, good and bad. Children are a natural outgrowth of love and commitment and are the responsibility of a community. Margaret perhaps has the "ideal" situation being able to parent without the day-to-day hassle that many full-time parents complain of. Her role, however, has in recent years been diminished, but "aunts" are valuable in the extended family community. They provide financial and emotional support and, in my view, need to be more incorporated into our traditional family unit.

Sharazad describes another successful extended family, which has always worked for us, and seemingly for her. She further describes some of the difficulties of raising Black boys (one of my closest friends talks of hiding her son in the bulrushes until he is 30). We have developed a habit of raising irresponsible men--we have to take some credit for that.

Jawanza Kunjufu writes, "some women raise their daughters and love their sons." When raising girls we make them responsible, decisive, and able to handle anything. Boys, on the other hand are encouraged to be just the opposite. We must realize that our children are on loan to us and our task is to raise adults who can make contributions to the community. Sharazad seems to have licked that problem with a five-year-old who "talks about his feelings" and knows that there are choices and consequences, good or bad, for his actions. She is on the right track.

"Anonymous, Detroit" outlines the traditional nuclear family. Mother, father and 2.5 children. While we ascribe to this, sometimes it works and sometimes it doesn't. Lucky for her and her life partner, it did. The things that are important to her and her family are shown in their activities, which clearly build self-esteem and a high likelihood of successful offspring. The only problem she probably has developed is trying to make things a little "too perfect." When that happens, we frequently forget about ourselves, putting others needs first. We need to remember to take care of ourselves first. We need to remember that in order to take care of others--we have to first take care of ourselves. I hope "Anonymous, Detroit" is doing so.

Similarly, Meryl highlights a very "common problem" with African American women and the very real likelihood of single parenting. Parenting is difficult enough and we frequently underestimate the stress of the day-to-day stuff, (compounded if you have more than one child). The biggest mistake we make is two-fold: not relying on an extended family (e.g., trying to do everything) and not taking time for yourselves. I encourage women to do just that--parenting is not a perfected science. We all need help, and we will make bad choices from time to time. We need to read, ask, and discover. We are not alone! But in order to do our best, we have to take the best care of ourselves--so that we can give more time to them. A concept called "PARENTIFICATION" (older children taking care of the younger) has historically worked for us and teaches responsibility early. One organization to try: the SISTERHOOD OF BLACK SINGLE MOTHERS (see "Resources") provides parenting support through newsletters, activities, etc.

However, Meryl seems somewhat confused about her role as mother. She can't be a "friend" to a ten-year-old child. She has to be a parent, not a sorority sister. I think it shows in her statement, "...perhaps I am trying to develop a friendship with her that I did not have with other girls in my childhood..." Meryl needs to resolve this issue by getting adult friends (see "Chapter Five") and relationships. She also needs to encourage her daughter to be involved with children her own age--even though she is mature for her age. The time for developing "friendships" with your children is when they are adults.

The greatest joy is seeing your adult children succeed as Marianne described. At this point we can develop different friendly adult relationships with them. We can be effective parents from beginning to end!

THE 1-2-3 OF IT

We need to:

1. Understand that all intimate relationships are process oriented that is developing and changing over time. There is a beginning and an ending.

2. Know that relationships require both partners to give 100 percent. It's not a 50-50 thing, and accept that we cannot change anyone in a relationship, we can only change ourselves.

3. Believe children are a natural outgrowth of love and commitment between a community of individuals.

CHAPTER 7

The Unemployed:
How Not to Become "Annette Love"!

> "...I am being paid to take care of my children. Therefore, I am going to raise the best kids possible. I'm good at my job..."
>
> *Christine Wakefield, mother*

In the fall of 1990, an article appeared in our local newspaper entitled "The Death of Somebody." Annette Love, a 29-year-old woman from our inner city, was murdered. She had become depressed and fallen into what Dr. Kunjufu calls, The "Chain Of Pain". She developed low self-esteem and depression, had several children, was on welfare, and involved in illegal activity. My rejoinder:

"...so you are depressed, what about? Why have you not returned to school to get your GED for gainful employment? Who was providing care and guidance for your five underage children while you were in a bar, not once but twice, that day? When do you have time to date a purported drug dealer?..." These are questions I would have asked Annette Love as an African American psychologist specializing in African American women's issues, particularly in the inner city. Questions I ask everyday.

Angrily, I see this "CHAIN of PAIN" frequently. Low self-esteem leads to teenage pregnancy, which leads to high school drop outs, which leads to unemployment and welfare, which leads to illegal activity (drugs/crime), and then prison or death. Needless to say, the "Chain of Pain" is very evident in Annette's short life.

I was horrified to discover that 65 percent, yes, 65 percent of our community is on aid of some kind to support themselves and their families. In fact, Milwaukee has the highest teenage-pregnancy rate in a metropolitan area in the country.

What will bring an end to this "CHAIN OF PAIN"? Self-esteem which provides the basis for the desire to graduate from high school, become gainfully employed, and succeed. Self-esteem will circumvent the problems of teenage pregnancy, unemployment, Black on Black crime, prison and early death for many of our community youth. Unfortunately, many successful Blacks leave to move to White neighborhoods where we cannot be effective role models.

I recently had two discrepant clients in my office in the same day. Both women's "M-O's" were identical to Annette's. The first client had a 15-year-old son who literally was on his way down. His mother had decided to begin parenting him within the last few months of what will probably be a short life span. "Late" I told her. The latter client realized early on that she wanted to do better and involved herself in supportive services (education, social intervention, etc.,). Guess which will have the more successful outcome?

I only wish Annette, realizing her worth and state of mind, had chosen not to go to a bar but had chosen a more empowering alternative as my latter client did. "Just in time," I could have told her.

Welfare mothers are frequently scorned by society. There is a misconception that there are more Black women on Aid to Families with Dependent Children (AFDC) than White women. Actually there are six White women to every Black woman on aid. These mothers always say they have lots of time on their hands; consequently, they consider raising their kids a full-time job. If you look at it that way, these women have 18 years in which to develop several careers--traditional and nontraditional. We should, as I would say, always be looking for a job or better opportunity. We have too many choices to settle for less.

The problem is we frequently think of our job situation in the traditional manner. African American women are overrepresented in the low paying jobs such as office workers, nurses and dietitians, social workers and elementary school teachers. We are underrepresented in high paying jobs such as computer scientists, doctors, and lawyers or nontraditional jobs, such as construction workers. In this chapter, I encourage women to become the best possible by using all the opportunities they have earned, including access to mental health care, education and like-supportive services.

> "...I've stopped looking for a job pretty much. The rejection factor just became too much. I want nice things, but I have never been able to afford them. I dropped out of high school to have my baby. At the time I thought that was okay. People say I should go back and get my GED, I just don't feel good enough about myself to do that..."
>
> *Janet, 22,*
> *single, mother, Des Moines*

> "...very unemployed..."
>
> *Mary, 43, single, sometime*
> *clerical temporary employee, Washington, D.C.*

"...I dropped out of school after three years, came home and had a baby much to my mother's disappointment. I see that it is impossible to make a decent living without a degree..."

Gigi, Chicago

"...I am presently unemployed as the result of an accident in February of 1989. I have begun to reevaluate whether all the time and money I made were worth it. I suffered severe nerve damage and impairment to my lower extremities and am presently involved in physical therapy...all of the doctors feel there is not too much more they can do for me, I believe in the power of prayer, and I'm going to go forward..."

Lynda, 37, single, New Jersey

"...I'm not unemployed, but I work with the unemployed. I work for the social services, and it is very depressing at times. There seems to be a whole subclass of people who have made this system their whole lives. They make it their business to try to beat the system. It seems to be a lot of very young people turning up their noses at jobs at McDonald's, and they continually go through these human service systems. But I've seen that the system is full of holes and a lot of useless spending is going on. To me, it is just another way to prove the metal chains may be off us, but the mental chains are just as strong. Welfare is slavery, drug programs are chains, and poverty is a deterrent...nothing will change until we become responsible for our actions..."

**Leona, 36, single,
social services worker, Brooklyn**

I show my patients that there is a way out, namely, beginning with self-esteem. In fact, it is the first rung up on the ladder of success.

Janet, Mary, Gigi, and Lynda all suffer from low self-esteem which has moved them down the ladder of success. (Annette has already hit rock bottom and lost her life, leaving five children motherless.) Janet, lacking self-esteem, is well on her way, having even stopped looking for a job because she doesn't feel good enough about herself. Gigi, also with a child, made the attempt to complete school, probably without a support system. Mary has gotten into the trap of "sometime employment," probably to tide her over in an emergency, in jobs that are mostly low paying such as clerical work. Lynda has gotten caught in the "disability trap"; believing the only job she can get is the one she can no longer do. We need to be more creative about our workspace.

Women living in poverty, or near poverty, have to survive unemployment, substandard housing, lack of health insurance, poor education, and inadequate nutrition, all of which contribute to poor mental health care. The focus of the day-to-day survival can manifest itself in psychiatric symptoms: helplessness, hopelessness, depression, alcohol and drug abuse, many of which Leona and myself have noted. Good medical and mental health care can change that, it is simply a matter of getting what you deserve.

I classify all of these women as the "ABLE DISABLED," giving up on life while they still have a chance to make it. They are "ABLE," but can't or refuse to do so and become "DISABLED." So many Black women give up; and worse, they give up at an early age. Janet, Mary, Gigi, and Lynda have a lot of life yet to live, but they don't feel good enough about themselves to do so.

For example, collecting disability or unemployment as Lynda does and then trying to maintain that "status" is a time waster! The situation with disability is that you are constantly called upon to verify your illness by making many trips to the doctor. You disagree with them, and you make a like number of visits to your attorney. Clearly, a circular journey that gets you nowhere fast and certainly not up the success ladder.

Climbing the success ladder and becoming "ABLE" involves first making and committing to changing your present unemployed situation. If you aren't committed to making a change, then you may as well stop reading right now!

Second, as Gigi discovered, it is important to get yourself into a support system, this might be family, friends, church, or a group of women that are trying to make a similar change. In fact, there is such a group called the NATIONAL BLACK WOMEN'S HEALTH PROJECT that can help you organize, or join an existing support group within your community. *(see Resources) One thing that African American women can do is gather together, talk, and problem solve.

Much of our self-esteem can be boosted from relying on one another as well as spending time on ourselves. I frequently have my clients begin at the beginning by reading the children's book by Dr. Seuss, Oh, the Places You'll Go and Tar Beach by Faith Ringold. Both talk about the rewards and difficulties of making necessary life changes. We can make these changes with help.

Another good guide is the Black Woman's Career Guide by Beatrice Nivens which talks about many different types of careers and the best way to get there.

The point is to begin thinking in different ways, because what we are doing now is not working--we have to try something else.

Once we are in a support system, we must continue to think in small goal-setting terms. Like Janet, if we don't have a high school diploma or GED we need to get one! This is essential--without it we will always be in menial, low paying service jobs as Mary discovered. Once in school, stay there. School is always a good place to grow. Whether it is taking a class for self enrichment, an apprenticeship or technical school, or college some knowledge is bound to be gained. Many of these offer financial aid and child care (which are two of the main reasons we don't go). I can't highlight enough the importance of continued learning throughout your entire life.

If we decide to stay in traditional work areas where we have always made money: at home (child care, food preparation, hair stylist), capitalize on it! Why not set up a home-based business and parlay it into a career? The NATIONAL BEAUTY CULTURISTS' LEAGUE (see Resources) helps black women get into the business of "doing hair." Similarly, the NATIONAL BLACK CHILD DEVELOPMENT INSTITUTE provides training in setting up a day care business or like services (see Resources). These are things we can already do--continue to stay at home, take care of our children, and develop or redevelop skills.

Another option you have is in a more nontraditional vein. Many jobs exist that pay well and offer on-the-job training or skills and opportunities in areas such as plumbing, protective services (police, fire), mechanics, and construction. Though the hours are long--and the work difficult--the pay is excellent. Organizations such as NONTRADITIONAL EMPLOYMENT FOR WOMEN, and WIDER OPPORTUNITIES FOR WOMEN (see Resources) based in New York and Washington, D.C., respectively, promote this type of employment for African American women in nontraditional jobs--and it is a clear cut way to break the cycle of unemployment and poverty.

While there may be broken "rungs" on the ladder to success, such as job discrimination and sexual harassment, many laws have been enacted to help us. There are things we can do today to overcome these problems. Groups like the Urban League and NAACP can offer support.

By developing self-esteem through a strong foundation (namely our support system) and getting further training, we can only increase our chances of succeeding. We can make a change and so can Janet, Mary, Lynda, and Gigi.

THE 1-2-3 OF IT

We need to:

1. Get ourselves into a support system be it
   family, friends, faith, or traditional
   psychotherapy, it is the basis of becoming
   employable.

2. Go back to school and stay there! We must,
   at the very least, have a GED to become
   employable. In fact, learning new things makes
   us feel good about ourselves and always
   employable. Skills and education make us
   marketable--in fact, we should always be
   looking for a job or better opportunity.

3. Make money now to break the cycle of poverty
   doing traditional things such as child care,
   doing hair or cooking. Later consider
   "nontraditional" jobs that will offer more
   opportunity-- and money.

Get to it!

CHAPTER 8

The Underemployed:
How can I Get Rid of Combat Fatigue?

> "...African American women deserve combat pay. Frequently isolated, emotionally abused, and overworked they get a case of combat fatigue for which they deserve combat pay..."
>
> *Juliette Martin, Ph.D., Psychologist*

Underemployed working mothers are frequently the ones who need the most help but are the least likely to receive it, because of the lack of time and access to care. They largely get support only when they need it, usually around a crisis. This "CRISIS-CENTERED LIFE-STYLE" means their lives function around crisis. In effect they become addicted to crises, their lives are built around crises, and their crises are built around their lives. They feel trapped and have learned that social, educational, and governmental agencies never give them what they need, so they must create other options. As a result, these individuals believe they have no control over their behavior and don't learn effective coping techniques.

Ann Petry's award winning novel *The Street*, tells the story of an African American mother and son, trying to make it. In the end, she gives up. These African American women frequently make bad choices (not mistakes) that are emotionally unhealthy or economically foolish. For example, if our employer misplaces our payroll check, he or she may look at it as a computer glitch, but this disrupts our life and we lose our internal locus of control. We may choose to kill someone over this, but that is a bad choice. Others may see this as antisocial, but we see it as our only choice.

As a result, "COMBAT FATIGUE" is a syndrome that is characterized by depression or moodiness (feeling sad), bouts of anger, problems sleeping, weight changes; or we may develop illnesses (e.g., lower back pain) due to stress or exacerbate illnesses that are common in our community (such as lupus or sickle cell anemia (see Resources). The women in this chapter have to learn effective coping skills, problem solving and decision making to better manage stress.

> "...I want to do better but I can't seem to get ahead. There is always a crisis..."
>
> *Airline, 38, married, waitress, Milwaukee*

"...frequently while on the line, I think I'm in slavery--true bondage. I am underemployed at GM, and I hate my job. I go to work everyday just to pay the bills..."

Roslyn, 32, separated,
line electrician, Flint

"...yes, I do consider myself underemployed. I work for an attorney. Last month he gave me a raise, which was $.48 added to my $7.00 only came up to a little bit over nothing...having little experience, I am now looking for a new job. I have worked three years in a law office but; experience will get me nowhere in the job market, even though I like working in the law field-- and am five units away from an associates degree in law (paralegal)--I still might have to look for a new field of work. This is what happens when you keep yourself underemployed..."

Shawn, 25, single,
secretary, Philadelphia

"...I am presently employed as a certification specialist. I interview people and determine their eligibility for program participation. It is a very stressful job. I believe most of the stress I am feeling is due, in part, to the mentality and morals of the majority of my clients. It is difficult working with clients who do not appear to have the same, or similar, mores as I. The other part of the stress is due to the mentality of my superiors. They seem to be operating with a plantation/overseer mentality. I am not at all happy in this position. As a result of this, I am both mentally and physically exhausted. The only thing good about this job is that I can provide life's basic needs for myself (food and shelter) and some of the frills (car and clothing). I am not happy with my job because I feel I am capable of doing better things and contributing to the quality of my fellow human beings lives for a lot more money. However, at this stage I am more cautious about "treading in uncharted waters..."

Shirley, 47, single,
certification specialist, Oakland

"...regarding your question 'Are you happily employed?' It makes me wonder what a happy employment situation is for Black women. I have defined being happily employed in two categories: money for financial needs to meet economic necessities and personal satisfaction. Before expressing my employment situation, I looked at other black women who have a common bond with my current employment situation. From counseling other black women that are nurses, waitresses, counselors, or factory workers, you learn their employment is based mostly on economic necessity. You find limited reasons for personal satis-faction. So knowing other black women has shown that economic necessities determines the major reasons for one being happily employed. After thinking about it, it has helped me to assess my employment situation. Since working in psychology as a counselor I have found personal satisfaction in helping people with their problems; for this reason, I am happily employed. I conclude that the interaction of personal satisfaction and economic necessity must exist in order for me to be happily employed..."

Ginger, 35, married,
counselor, Nashville

Ginger and I agree that these women need to recognize they have a "CRISIS-CENTERED LIFE-STYLE", and consequently, suffer from the symptoms of "COMBAT FATIGUE." They are literally fighting for and with everyone in their lives. Roslyn, Shawn, and particularly Shirley outline the problem well. Airline states that she "can't get ahead." Roslyn and Shirley talk of their situation as "slavery or bondage." If you think that you hate metal chains, the mental chains are surely worse. Shawn has somewhat of a key. It may be just the matter of her returning to school to get her associate's degree as a paralegal. This change may mean the difference in salary and certainly her state of mind. She will feel less trapped and will be able to make sane decisions about her life. In fact, with the right support system (e.g., NATIONAL ASSOCIATION OF BLACK WOMEN LAWYERS (see Resources), she may feel so confident about the decision that she might decide to become a full-fledged attorney! More difficult, Shirley described her situation, "...the stress I am feeling is due to the mentality of my superiors...they are operating at a plantation/overseer mentality...as a result of this I feel mentally and physically exhausted...." She is not alone in her feelings. Many of us struggle with this situation because as she says, "I can provide for myself life's basic needs (food and shelter)..." We are, for the most part, responsible people, who are responsible to the families that depend on us--which is one reason we stay. Another reason is found at the end of Shirley's letter, "I feel I am capable of doing better things and contributing to the quality of my fellow human beings lives, for a lot more money. However, at this stage I am more cautious about treading in uncharted waters..."

That is where learning effective coping techniques (stress management), problem solving, and decision making is important. Shirley needs to do several things. First, she needs to better cope with her present work situation. One option is to talk to others in her situation to see how they might handle things. It is also not inappropriate for her to speak to her bosses--slavery is over--and perhaps her bosses need to be reminded. There is no reason to "withstand an intolerable situation." Physically, she should take care of herself--that means a healthy diet and exercise. Mentally, it means time for herself and regard for just getting through the day. I encourage women to spend an hour doing something they want to do. That may mean taking a nap, watching Oprah, or anything as long as it is time spent on you. One thing we know about stress is that this recipe for stress management always works. If Shirley has children, it is even more crucial for her to have a regular routine, support, and above all take care of herself.

This will help in the short term, and the symptoms of "COMBAT FATIGUE" will subside. In the long term, however, she needs to problem solve and make some decisions about her life. Decision making is frequently scary for many of us because we feel we may make a mistake. In actuality, we need to re-frame it as a choice. We can make another one if need be. There are no mistakes! The easiest way to make choices in our lives is to gather as much information regarding those choices as possible--the more information we gather, the better decisions we can make. We may even go as far as writing these choices down, ranking them, etc. Whatever the system, the more decisions we make the better we get at it, and the more comfortable we will be in making them. This goes for Shirley as well. Like Roslyn, the choice to leave a job is difficult: but if we feel like slaves then, it is time to go. We should always be looking for our next opportunity or job. We should not stay because of pay and benefits, that truly is slavery. We don't need that. We can make changes in our lives.

Take this situation for example: one of my clients, while working two jobs to make ends meet, developed lupus (an ailment common in African Americans that causes joint swelling and subsequent pain) which of course was exacerbated and threw her out of the work situation for several months. While she worked, her son had become a problem in school. She had developed, in addition to the lupus, all sorts of other physical symptoms. She was literally suffering from "COMBAT FATIGUE" and felt as though she was in combat and under stress. She also felt particularly stressed because she was a college-educated woman--a four-year degree--and worked as a secretary for a governmental agency. She had begun to believe that she had no options--when in fact she did. She figured that out as soon as she developed lupus (a hidden blessing!)

and was forced to relax, spend more time with her son and take a good look at her work situation--and problem solve regarding it. She is now working one job 8-6. She made a good choice.

Look at what this contributor did:

"...I am presently working as a sales assistant/office manager for an insurance company. I am not happy in this job, and I do consider myself underemployed. The reason for my unhappiness is that I now know I can do more mentally. However, due to my lack of a four-year degree I have to stay in this position. I don't think I received the proper guidance growing up in reference to education, four-year colleges, or careers. I went to a two-year college because that is what I was exposed to. I was told that this would ensure me a job and get me the skills I would need. This was misleading, and now I am suffering for this. I wish I had known to go to a four-year college to teach, become a nurse, or even a doctor. These choices were never presented in my senior year when the business schools came and gave their presentations. I cannot remember other universities or colleges visiting or even the guidance counselor suggesting other alternatives. I think this lack of guidance and direction led me to gain a menial education and get into a low paying, dead-end job. I think that society puts us where they want us. However, I do not plan to stay in this position. I registered to attend a four-year college and change professions. I want to become a teacher and a positive-black role model for our children and give them the guidance which was not given to me. In the interim, I am taking better care of myself emotionally and physically. I am also contemplating working as a child care provider out of my home. This would help me change careers and then, when I have completed my education, I will have the experience in education to either open a day care or work as a teacher in a school...I plan to reach my goal before I am 35..."

Deidra, 27, married,
administrative assistant, Buffalo

Deidra has followed the steps of initially taking better care of her mind and body, generating interim and long-term choices for herself. She did it, we can too!

THE 1-2-3 OF IT

We need to:

1. Recognize our "CRISIS-CENTERED LIFE-STYLE" (our lives function around crises) and this causes "COMBAT FATIGUE" physical and emotional-e.g. depressive symptoms that make us tired).

2. Learn effective "COPING SKILLS" such as "STRESS MANAGEMENT"; (healthy, diet and exercise).

3. Learn "PROBLEM SOLVING" and "DECISION MAKING"--make choices, not mistakes.

CHAPTER 9

The Employed:
How not to be the "Only One!"

> "...I have a foot in each world, but I cannot fool myself about either...I am burdened daily with showing Whites that Blacks are people. I am a "credit to my race"...I am my sister's keeper though many of them have abandoned me because they think I have abandoned them..."
>
> *Leanita McClain, Journalist*

You've made it. BMW. MBA. A company woman. Maybe even a MRS. The trappings of success are everywhere around you. However, you look around and see you're the "ONLY ONE." That's okay because everyone says that you have arrived. You're happy or so you think you're happy--but you ask yourself that a little too frequently. To keep yourself in check, it seems as though you have had to develop two separate personalities. A "Black one" and unfortunately "a corporate one" (White one). What you've got is "ETHNIC SCHIZOPHRENIA." Ethnic schizophrenia develops when we try to ascribe to their standard of behavior, which means we have to have two ways of interacting with our friends at home and at work. What it means is reproving ourselves to both groups over and over and over--much like resetting the high bar and jumping again and again. Worse, we have found it is twice as difficult to get there (be successful), and three times as hard to stay there, which makes us, in a sense, crazy. The people that we work with say we are "not like other Blacks" and the people at home say "We are not the way we used to be--"Too much booklearning." The women in this chapter are clearly suffering from this malady. Confusing, because after all we should be happy we've made it! Or have we?

> "...I have got to be twice as good just to keep my job, more if I want to be promoted. This is to say nothing of fitting in the needs of my family..."
>
> *Betty, 32, married,*
> *bank vice-president, Dallas*

> "...Black folks are called arrogant on the job, whites confident..."
>
> *Michelle, 37, married,*
> *IBM executive, Boston*

"...I am not happily employed, and I do not think I have a very fulfilling career. I am overqualified educationally for the full-time position I hold currently. I realize that this is not uncommon for Black women to be overqualified. I have a master's degree in English. Although I am good at what I do, I know I am capable of doing more challenging work. I am the only Black female employed at the company. As the only Black woman here, I feel isolated. I don't have anyone who would understand my experiences. I think my actions and decisions, particularly as they apply to editing, are questioned because I am Black and female..."

Anonymous, Seattle

All of these women underline the stress of being the "ONLY ONE." Both Betty and Michelle note that being Black and the best is a liability not an asset in White corporate America (more aptly described race representative, good employee not like the others, "TWOFER" see "Chapter 4"). Michelle is particularly sensitive to that--hence her confidence factor.

As I have stated before, we are very used to working. It is also a truism that we have to be twice as good or "overqualified"--as our "Anonymous" contributor from Seattle noted. In effect, the better we are at our jobs the more trapped we may feel--trapped from our support system and stuck at that "glass ceiling" that frequently keeps us being the "ONLY ONE" in our company.

A vignette from the play "The Colored Museum" by George Wolfe illustrates the problem well: In "symbiosis" the characters describe the pain of having to give up all of their African American traditions throwing out all their "rhythm and blues" albums and books (e.g., Temptations, and Eldridge Cleaver's *Soul on Ice*), a dashiki, hair products, and, of course, their home in the neighborhood.

The character states,

"...being Black is too emotionally taxing; therefore, I will be Black only on weekends and holidays..."

A shocking statement but all too true. Some of us will change the radio station in our car when we approach work, wear the ascribed clothing, or decorate our offices in a corporate socially appropriate way (e.g., no sign of an African American here), etc. This only adds to our confusion. Perhaps the most compelling and painful example of this phenomenon is the death of Leanita McClain, an editor of the *Chicago Tribune* newspaper. At the age of 32, she committed suicide in part related to her living an "ETHNIC SCHIZOPHRENIC" life. She often wrote about the pain of being the "ONLY ONE" in her work place, and having to write about the range of problems and positives in the African American community. She sometimes apologized for the state of her people as though she were personally responsible for them. She, of course, took criticism from the Black community because she was quick to point out these inadequacies. The White community saw her as a "black girl done good." She and her husband, Clarence Page (also from the Tribune), moved up the career ladder quickly and moved north from the neighborhood. (She had been born and raised in the projects.) She increasingly became depressed, her marriage failed, and she eventually committed suicide. The pressure of her schizophrenic life had simply become too much.

Leanita had in fact "failed" the three lessons of this chapter. How then do we counteract this problem of being "successful?"

One place to start is to listen to the following contributor:

"...I'm a 27-year-old black woman professionally employed in corporate America. The position I hold as a writer for a major newspaper has been a source of frustration because of conflicts created by the institutional structure itself. I have worked hard to challenge and handle conflicts. I went into journalism hoping to make a difference and to help educate the public about the important issues. I have encountered difficulties along the way as I attempted to write progressive, Africentric stories that challenged the status quo. To my dismay, I have learned that many of the so-called intelligent and professional people that I have worked with are working to keep the status quo intact. A series of experiences in the business have shown me that racism and sexism remain strong forces that potentially degenerate Black people (who make up only a few in the corporate setting). I have become extremely angry, frustrated and depressed about these situations involving injustices and unfairness that are caused by institutionalized racism. It has been a struggle to maintain my dignity and ethnic pride in a system that is structured to make people conform to the corporate way. It has been my belief in a universal truth of a supreme being and connectedness that has helped me survive and keep my sanity. Corporate America is very difficult on Black people for a number of reasons. The system expects us to conform to rules and respect policies that often restrict our personal and professional growth. I have refused to keep mum on matters that are crucial to speak out about. I understand more than ever the truth, the threat, and the vulnerability I'm faced with as a result of openly challenging racist and sexist practices. But I am willing to take those risks. I have worked hard on soul-searching, developing the inner strength for coping with insane and unjust practices. I have no choice but to speak up if I want to live with myself..."

Rosemary, 27, single, journalist, Washington, D.C.

Journalist or not, Rosemary speaks for many of us that have had success but felt trapped, very trapped: "...I have encountered difficulties along the way as I attempted to write progressive Africentric stories that challenged the status quo..." Interpretation? I must apologize for the media interpretation of all African Americans!!! Wrong. No apologies necessary. Remember we must maintain our personhood-that means represent yourself first and foremost. Rosemary is only responsible for writing stories, Africentric or not, that she chooses and that are of interest to her public. She need not feel that she has to right all the wrongs of the media and how they portray us, or worse, apologize for how diverse the African American community is. We are not a monolithic group! African Americans come in all shapes and sizes and from all economic backgrounds and educational levels. We buy into the media's image of an impoverished, uneducated group of people. (Remember the example of the Cosby Show, we were the first ones to say such a family--doctor, lawyer and children doing well in school--could not possibly exist in our community.)

"...it has been a struggle to maintain my ethnic pride in a system that racism and sexism is structured to make people conform to the corporate way..." Like the general society, we have been socialized to believe that the corporate way is the best way. Rosemary needs to keep her own identity. That may mean decorating her office in an ethnic way, wearing ethnic clothes, listening to our music, whatever it takes--she is a contributor to the whole and needs to be seen as such--the whole being corporate America. There is no reason to "give up ourselves" because of a job that we are at eight hours a day. Switching back and forth between two personalities is, in effect, exhausting. Do not fall prey to stereotypes (e.g., race representative). This frequently happens because we have been socialized to believe that there is a "good" way of acting. There is a correct way of behaving within the corporate structure certainly, however, that does not mean being the "housenigger."

Lastly, Rosemary says:

"...I have no choice but to speak up if I want to live with myself..."

Hurrah! Rosemary realizes that she is the "ONLY ONE" of her, and that is special. Her issues need to be out on the table for all to see. Many times we as African Americans prefer to sweep things under the rug to fit into the corporate mold. Nothing could be further from the truth. It is the specialness that makes us unique and certainly makes our self-esteem soar.

We need to become more creative about our workspace and not think in terms of a job but our lives. Not a job but a lifestyle that is more fulfilling. We need to think in terms of "they are lucky to have us" as employees, so that we can begin to feel more in control of our lives, and that means a workspace that is comparable to us! One of the things that we don't think about is banning together into our own organizations within corporations. Many professional groups such as the NATIONAL ASSOCIATION FOR BLACK SOCIAL WORKERS and the NATIONAL ASSOCIATION FOR BLACK NURSES have support systems within their ranks. Other groups such as the NATIONAL BAR ASSOCIATION, the NATIONAL DENTAL ASSOCIATION, and the NATIONAL MEDICAL ASSOCIATION have formed their own support organizations as well. Engineers, accountants, and probably every other professional career has one also. If not, we need to start one. Ongoing workshops, groups, and helpful information regarding being the "ONLY ONE" are available (see Resources). A great book to read is the *Minority Executive's Handbook* by Randolph Cameron. Being successful does not mean selling out!

THE 1-2-3 OF IT

We need to:

1. Maintain our personhood. Represent ourselves first and foremost, make sure you get yourself into a good support system with other "Only Ones."

2. Do Not fall prey to stereotypes: (e.g., race representative).

3. Remember that each of us is unique; there is "ONLY ONE" of you.

Many of us wish we could become entrepreneurs, but we are afraid to take the plunge.

Chapter 10

Entrepreneurs:
How can I Make my Dreams Come True?

"For a lot of people, I recognize that I carry their dreams. When they see me they see themselves, and it is all right for me to make $1 million or $2 million because they can conceive of themselves making a million. They can't conceive making $30 or $50 million, it's too much."

Oprah Winfrey, actress/talk show host.

Power, the kind that choice and money bring, has been a scary thing for Black women. Will it alienate me from my family? my community? What if I fail? I asked myself all of these questions when I decided to launch out on my own. I too, was "employed" with good benefits, but I felt that I could do more for my community. The final straw was when my chairman came to me and said, "We have to harness your creativity." At that point, I knew I had to be on my own making a contribution, not only to myself, but to my community. Limiting my practice to African American women was my first step, this book was the second, the third? Well, we'll see. It is the fact that I can choose.

Many times African American women often limit their choices and opportunities as outlined in Ms. Winfrey's quote, and I'm sure she went through similar choices as I did. Part of the specialness of our race and sex is that we are adept at making many, many, many choices, what I like to call effective "Cultural Switching": getting what you want from majority society--more on that later. In effect we have had our own businesses (as I said in Chapter Seven) when we watched children, cooked food for others or "did hair." Traditionally, these businesses have flourished in the Black community. Consequently, we have too many options to limit ourselves. Remember we make choices every day: whether to react to a racist comment, or go to our child's school over a problem, or how we are going to interact with our mate. We can make the same choices about our work life. Many of us wish we could become entrepreneurs but we are afraid to take the plunge at being self-employed--all too used to regular vacations and pay checks. The letters in this chapter highlight women in the process of choosing entrepreneurship.

"...I have written a business plan for a men's clothing store/mail order business, featuring clothing for the larger man, appealing to the traditional 'big and tall,' the athlete and most of the African American male population, since their bodies have very different proportions than the white male. The problem I am having is money and a supportive group of friends or business associates to work with. I really need a 'mentor' type of person that I could bounce ideas off from time to time. But I am unable to locate such a person..."

Anonymous, California

"...during my maternity leave, December 1988 through June 1989, I received a master's degree in public administration. I then decided a well- established, home-based business was my best source of stable income. To initiate the process of becoming a management consultant, I took classes. I have read background materials (books and articles from past issues of Essence magazine on established role models have been extremely beneficial), developed a business plan/goal, established a work area, stocked supplies (business cards, office supplies, typewriter, answering machine), done network marketing and read articles on time management. I am all ready to go except for two small important people--a 21-month-old son and a daughter almost eight...how can I be totally successful at both home management and a home-based business without jeopardizing the business or my children's nurturing?..."

Violet, 40, married, Poughkeepsie

"...I am not happily employed. I have been a speech-language pathologist for 16 years. I have reached burnout. My case load is comprised of 70 students with various handicapping conditions. I am responsible for implementing therapy as well as insurmountable paperwork. I was the first African American speech pathologist hired in a predominately small, white, middle to upper-middle class suburban community. I had to work twice as hard to prove my worth. When I married, I moved to Norfolk, Virginia, where I was employed for five years as a speech-language pathologist. During the year of 1979, I served five schools in one week. After my divorce, I returned to the same county I resigned from. During the first four years of divorce, the school I worked at had students who were physically, mentally, and emotionally impaired. I realize now in 1990, I want to be an entrepreneur. My need for a complete career change is greater now than it ever was..."

Deborah, 45, divorced, nine-year-old son,
speech pathologist, Baltimore

"...YES! YES! YES! I would like to be able to live off my earnings as a writer. However, right now I have decided to put that goal on hold for a few years. I still write. It just isn't a top priority at this time. I would also like to have a bookstore cafe--a coffee house type place. It is essential to me that this be in an African-American community. I am sure there is at least one somewhere in this country unknown to me..."

Katherine, 28, engaged,
youth counselor, Minneapolis

"...I am an entrepreneur! I have owned and operated a specialty shop (Big Legs and Pretty Things) for three years--haven't made any money yet, but I'm keeping the doors open!..."

Delores, Milwaukee

So much of our lives is under our control, and as we see from this set of letters many of us don't believe that it is. Many of us believe that a regular paycheck and benefits are signs of success--they are if you want to limit yourself. Entrepreneurship is reserved for those of us who want to make a difference. Becoming an entrepreneur gives us more choices.

Oprah made that choice and has developed effective "CULTURAL SWITCHING," but the world is full of "Oprahs." "Cultural Switching" is the ability to get what you want from majority society without selling out. Knowing the system, so to speak. All of these women are in various stages of entrepreneurship: 1) making a decision that you are tired of the "9 to 5," 2) developing a product, 3) research and marketing--developing a business plan and financing, 4) finding a mentor, 5) preparing a time line (when you are ready to make the job change), and 6) launching out on your own including company name, location, licensing and insurance if need be.

Deborah is clearly at the beginning of making a decision to change her workspace. Many of us after working a job for a long time realize that it is no longer fulfilling all of our needs. Similarly Katherine has made a choice, but decided to defer action on her plan. Violet and "California" have made the decision, and have even come up with plans, but have pieces missing: for "California" it is a mentor figure which is crucial to any entrepreneurial enterprise; Violet has a similar problem--little or no support system. Both need to obtain needed support, mostly through mentoring. Violet may need to rely on her life partner till she is off the ground and can make other arrangements for child care. Having your own business is working! Delores is well on her way. She knows the system and is ultimately using it to her advantage. In comparing IQ scores, African Americans typically score higher on performance tests--that is because we have become adept at making moment-to-moment decisions (as Delores has) all the time. Consequently, we are good at making effective choices. Empowerment is more than within our reach.

Look at these statistics for example: there are approximately 30 million African Americans in the country--12 percent of the population. This segment contributes a combined annual income of $300 billion to the economy. The total number of African American businesses have all increased in the last decade from 339,039 to about 400,000 between 1982 and 1989, but it is still disproportionately small. In the ten-year survey of business trends in review of the Black economy, only 21 percent of African American entrepreneurs reported having parents or relatives who were or had been in business. This contrasted with nearly 40 percent of White male entrepreneurs.

How then does one succeed at entrepreneurship? Back to the lesson plan: first, choose to become self-employed. It means a life-style change. A good place to start is to ask yourself these questions:

1. Do I want to do better?

2. Can I make a commitment (including sacrifices) for something I believe in?

3. Do I have a good support system?

4. Do I have something to say and/or something to sell?

5. Am I savvy enough to get backing, funding, etc.?

The more yeses you have, the more "entrepreneurability" you have, and the more success you will have. If you do well here it is essential that you develop a support system. It can be family and friends, but a better choice is to work with mentors (people or organizations that are related to the business you are trying to develop). Several options include: the AMERICAN INSTITUTE FOR ECONOMIC DEVELOPMENT, the COALITION OF MINORITY WOMEN IN BUSINESS, MINORITY BUSINESS INFORMATION INSTITUTE, and the NATIONAL ASSOCIATION FOR BLACK WOMEN ENTREPRENEURS, or your local or NATIONAL ASSOCIATION OF BLACK and MINORITY CHAMBERS OF COMMERCE (see Resources). Talk to as many people as possible, network, and read everything you can get your hands on related to entrepreneurship. Again, an excellent guide is the book by Beatrice Nivens, *The Black Woman's Career Guide*. Next devise and revise a business plan and financial backing. Last, of course, is launching out on your own. Don't be afraid to downscale your goals or revise the plan at any time. You may even want to do a final run of your idea. Remember it may take a few years to reap the benefits of your investment so it is crucial to be prepared. Now you're ready to go forth. If you have come this far, remember you are bound to make it. You can make a difference.

In fact, you can be a part of the change to encourage more Black enterprise and entrepreneurship which must be instilled early on. The educational system should provide guidance, however, public schools are not geared to challenging young people, let alone getting African American young people into business. This is a problem for career counselors across the nation. African American entrepreneurs find that they must go beyond the Black community because they get so little support from other Blacks. Even though African Americans spend $300 billion a year, only seven percent of it goes to Black-owned businesses. This absence of revenue not only limits the growth of Black businesses but also reduces the community's economic clout. To have any impact on the larger business community, Black businesses must first draw a larger percentage of the Black consumer dollars. African Americans have been subtly taught that only individuals coming from the dominant cultures have the skills needed to produce quality goods and services. It is a mind-set that has proven to be very difficult to overcome. One reason has been the absence of African American role models and images in the mass media, up until the last 25 years. For example, it's only recently that a show such as "The Cosby Show" could have existed, and as I said earlier, when it did exist, African Americans were quick to say, "This is not real black life." To keep Black spending dollars within the Black community, businesses must convince consumers that the goods and services available in Black communities are equal in quality to those they now often purchase in White communities one place to start is the "Black Pages" (listing of Black businesses and services) available in most metropolitan areas. We have got to learn to buy back and buy Black! This is just the beginning--because we can mentor and support others through the process and it's reinforcing for us as well. We can make a change for ourselves and our community together!

THE 1-2-3 OF IT

We need to:

1. Choose entrepreneurship. Remember it's reserved for those who are tired of collecting only a paycheck and benefits and who want to make a difference in their lives as well as others.

2. Talk to people, particularly anyone who has a similar idea or prior experience (mentor) in your area. Contact your local Minority Small Business Association, Chamber of Commerce, or like organization.

3. Devise and revise a business plan. Research your market thoroughly before launching out. Don't be afraid to make changes and celebrate any successes.

CHAPTER 11

The ABC's of Empowerment

So frequently in my practice I see this same pattern: unexpressed feelings, nonassertive behavior, and poor self-concept. Solving the problem can be as simple as re-learning your ABC's. Even though many African American women need good mental health care, they are the least likely to get it. This is primarily due to irrational ideas such as: 1) "I don't want anybody in my business," 2) "Psychotherapy is for white women--

I have my faith, family, and friends to talk about my problems with," or worse, 3) "I don't have that kind of time to spend on myself." These are just some of the ideas that must be dismantled before African American women can become more empowered and take responsibility for their own happiness. Though many of these ideas have been bantered about within traditional psychotherapy circles, we have not believed they applied to us--they do. That is what EMPOWERMENT, our EMPOWERMENT, is all about. Many people, women in particular, run from power because they confuse it with an aggressive description. Women in power are usually seen as difficult but frankly shouldn't be. As a result we continue not to understand it. First of all, there is a difference between personal and professional power. Power actually means choices and control. Personal power exists when you feel good about yourself and in control of events about your life. For example, if you're undergoing a divorce that's difficult it's not the end of the world but an opportunity to make life changes. Personal power is the power within, the power to do things--make a difference in your life.

Professional power is more an earned responsibility. It's most apparent in your job situation when people have some control over your job to some degree. The more choices and control you have--the more power. Here is a brief quiz to help decide if you have personal and professional power:

Professional Power

1. Do I have choices in my job situation, such as work area, projects, and so forth?

2. If I left my job tomorrow would I know what I wanted to do?

3. Do I get what I want, for example, memos typed or responses to requests I make?

4. Do I influence personnel?

Personal Power

1. If a traumatic event occurs what will be my long-term response? (i.e., will my life be over?)
2. Do I feel good about myself most of the time?
3. Do I feel I have control over my destiny?
4. Am I nice to myself?
5. Do I express myself regularly?

The more yeses you have the more personal (and professional power you have).

The first part of the lesson is learning about AFFECT, or feelings. Most women can't identify their feelings much less know what to do with them. Our feelings can be broken down into four categories MAD, GLAD, SAD, and SCARED.

A! IS FOR AFFECT.

Mad

Affect simply means feelings. One of the things African American women don't do is express feelings or express them in an inappropriate fashion, neither, of course, gets our needs met. For example, Cynthia, a 40-year-old broker frequently feels out of control when she is at work. "It was not just the environment that's stressful, but I frequently felt that I was going to explode if I got angry at something and felt that I would have to kick a wall in or beat someone up, so I just didn't get angry." Anger is probably the scariest concept for African American women to understand. We usually tend to act it out in an aggressive fashion, such as what Cynthia was doing, though we need to understand that anger is a feeling and not a behavior. We can be angry without "going off on someone." The expression of anger is like a safety valve, something that we need to do, to let off steam so that we can get on with our lives. Just as we express to someone that we love them, we can do the same with being angry. We can compare how we usually handle anger to a teapot stewing on the back of the stove; if we don't remove some of the pressure sooner or later, it boils over.

A bigger problem is that because we hold our anger inside then explode, we usually feel very guilty because as African American women being angry is a bad thing. We are the eternal "soothers," "comforters," and "smoother-overs." The key or trick is to learn how to express our feelings, particularly anger, on a "case-by-case" basis expressing how we are feeling at any given time, and NOT FEELING GUILTY ABOUT IT. Because we have been socialized not to express our anger, this is difficult for us to unlearn.

One of the things that I usually instruct my clients to do is to first begin to identify how it feels to be angry. Cynthia described feeling "out of control." Other women might say that they feel their stomach is upset or they have headaches or heart palpitations; once you have identified the feeling, the trick is then to express the feeling and begin to feel comfortable doing so. Many times we will say, "If I get angry then people won't like me anymore," "My family will disown me," "My husband will leave me," or "My kids won't respect me." All of which is untrue. (Also untrue is that if someone is related to us, they will "do right by us." People are people and will do you wrong.) Your feelings should be important to your family and friends; and if you are unable to express these feelings, then you probably need to reevaluate the relationship.

Glad

Being happy is probably the easiest feeling to identify, but we also tend to feel guilty when we are happy. After all, everyone else around us is miserable! Sharon, a 31-year-old housewife, had become content in her new life. She was a homemaker, had a small child, and her husband appeared to be loving and supportive of her desire to remain at home. Her working friends, however, said that she had become "complacent," didn't know "what was going on in the world around her," and began to actually make Sharon believe that she was unhappy because she had chosen this as her life path. We can't let this continue to happen! African American women have more choices, perhaps, than any other group. That's primarily because we have been in and worked in so many different settings. One of the settings in which we have not usually had the opportunity to spend luxury time is at home--we have had to fit work around it. If Sharon's desire is to do that and be happy, it can be that simple. It is totally under our control. Doing something good for ourselves, regardless of how small it is, can bring about feeling glad or feeling happy. For me, it is taking an afternoon nap with one of my cats, Elizabeth.

Sad

Depression is often expressed as anger turned inward. It is easier for us as African American women to be depressed and admit it. Ann, a client, told me once, "I have been depressed so long I am afraid of what will happen when I let loose, I'll probably kill myself. It is easier for me to say I'm sad, it's more acceptable to my family and friends." Ann displays so typically what women feel who have been unable to express anger. Many women appear in my office depressed because it is a lot easier admitting that you are depressed--it is more acceptable in other words. What Ann and others need to learn is to express their feelings on an ongoing basis. They will feel more in control and will be more likely to get their needs met. Not only do we not express our feelings, we don't ask for the things that we need because we feel undeserving, that has got to stop! Scared

Being scared is more difficult to define, because it may include feelings that you are uncomfortable with. African American women have been socialized to believe that we are "fearless." We take care of so many things and so many people without saying it is too much, we tend to be afraid to say "enough is enough." I remember a client telling me that she didn't know that she was scared. She was balancing an incredible load and afraid that she would fail. She was a corporate attorney working 60 or 70 hours a week, managing a household, being there for all of her friends and a demanding mother. This is very, very common. Many women, Black women in particular, continue to handle a multitude of things for a multitude of people being afraid to say "NO, I AM TIRED; I CAN'T DO ANY MORE!" We may also be more afraid to appear as failures. In this instance, we have got to accept that being a "failure" is more than acceptable. Unless we can make sure our needs are met, we can't meet anyone else's needs. We need to become "NUMBER ONE," in other words.

B IS FOR BEHAVIOR!

Given our difficulty with feelings, the next step of our lesson-- behavior--becomes even more important. Our behavior can be broken into three areas: NONASSER-TIVE, AGGRESSIVE, AND ASSERTIVE. Most often African American women are nonassertive or passive at home for a variety of reasons: we have been taught to be nonassertive and super supportive to our men or other relationships (after all, once we have this man we may not get another). Conversely, we tend to be very aggressive at work, particularly if we feel that racism is involved. We can "go off" in a minute. Unfortunately, neither of these scenarios gets our needs met.

Nonassertive

Most women have been socialized to be nonassertive--nice, that is. Nonassertiveness means not being able to state your feelings and make requests. Sheila, a 26-year-old accountant, thought being nice would ultimately make people like her. Unfortunately, it did not work quite that simply. People, particularly her family and friends, took advantage of her; and she felt more and more depressed and angry. She wrote, "I felt like a doormat." This is a very, very common syndrome many women believe--the nicer they are the nicer other people will be toward them. What happens instead is, we end up not being very nice to ourselves. Additionally, others see us as targets for getting their needs met. We commonly associate saying NO with being not so nice, and we certainly were taught. What we need to learn is to be nice to ourselves first, and if we feel like it, nice to others as well. Quite a difference!

Aggressive

African American women are more often aggressive, particularly at work, because it seems more acceptable in our community to "blow up." If we are in a situation that seems racially motivated, we are likely not to tolerate it, particularly in our work situation. Nancy, an 18-year-old pre-med student, describes it best this way, "I try not to be angry because I usually end up hitting someone." As I have described anger, the same applies here. Anger is a feeling; aggression is a behavior. You can get angry without hitting someone. The outcome need not be aggressive behavior. Aggressive behavior only begets aggressive behavior and that is not what you want.

Assertive

Assertiveness is simply a learned skill in which women learn to express their feelings (e.g., mad, glad, sad, scared) and make requests (I don't want you to do that anymore). Kathy, a 36-year-old secretary, describes her transition to becoming assertive. "I began to express my feelings and make requests. I got my needs met for the most part and I'm a lot happier." It can be that simple--but remember this is a learned skill and you are apt to forget to be assertive. That's okay, like any other learned skill it is never too late to back track. It is also okay not to be assertive if you choose to. You have the choice to be aggressive, nonassertive, or assertive. You simply need to know the consequences for each. For example, nonassertive behavior will ultimately lead to depression and fear, aggressive behavior to aggression, and assertiveness to happiness, of course.

C! is for SELF-CONCEPT

Marita Golden, describing the first day of school for one of her characters in her novel *A Woman's Place,* noted about our self-esteem: "Reminds me how my mama used to warn me not to put my hands on anything in the homes of those people she cleaned house for. I always wondered what my hands would do to those mirrors and dishes their hands wouldn't. And as I got closer to my class room I wondered what I could learn in a building like that was going to save me. Because that is what my mama told me education was suppose to do. Anyway, the feeling I got walking through that building, down those halls, sank into my skin and made me sick. I think I felt that way because I couldn't find anything there that made me think of me. By the time I got to the classroom, my hands were all sweaty and the muscles in my stomach were in a knot so tight I almost had cramps. I looked in and saw over 100 students. I saw an empty seat for me and not another black face. Then, without even thinking about it, this feeling like this is what I had to do I turned around and walked back to the entrance...I knew they didn't see me, and I knew I didn't care..."

Externally Defined

A good thing has happened in the African American community. Words and phrases like EMPOWERMENT, TAKING RESPONSIBILITY, and IMPROVING SELF-ES-TEEM have all become part of our vernacular. Consequently, our self-concept can become more internally defined, rather than externally defined. Up until now, it has been the other way around. Externally defined is when we allow the media and the public at large to define us, which are largely White. An internally defined self-concept is when we choose to define ourselves, which until recently we have been unable to do. For example, African American children watch more television than any other group; and as we all know most of the images on television are White. African American children then begin to internalize and believe that to be successful, powerful, and educated you have to have blond hair and blue eyes.

Look at what we have done to our hair, for example. We have gone through "naturals," heat treatments, chemicals, braids, and now weaves as if we were trying to find our identity. Now I am not against any of these hair styles (God knows I have used enough chemicals!) but these are the images the media have given us--what is an appropriate hair style? We need to do the defining!

If we are seen as having "overcome," African Americans are usually seen as super heroes--a phrase I frequently call "super Negro." White individuals will usually accept me because of my degree and stature in the community. However, the flip side of that is that I am no longer seen as an African American, instead I'm seen as someone who has "overcome" her blackness. Again, that is an externally defined self-concept. As another example, while seeing patients in the hospital, frequently I am mistaken for a nurse, social worker, or secretary--never Dr. Hicks. Not that I have anything against these professions--the larger point is that we are still not seen routinely as doctors, dentists, attorneys, etc. We still have a long way to go to change these perceptions, even within our own community.

Internally Defined

An internally defined self concept is when we choose to define ourselves which we have been unable to do until recently. Feeling good about ourselves really defines who we are, where we are going and the best way to get there. Linda, a 30-year-old dentist, never felt good about herself on the inside; consequently, she would say that many people didn't like her or would respond negatively to her.

Many people can come up with negative things to say about themselves, but usually they can't come up with positive things. We need to be able to generate a list of positive things about ourselves instantaneously. I suggest that we even go so far as to write the list down and keep it with us or tape it up on the mirror to review from time to time. If we can see positive things in ourselves, then others can see positive things in us as well and treat us as we deserve to be treated.

There is a major difference between self-love and selfishness. Selfishness connotes taking care of "Number 1" to the exclusion of all others, in addition to not caring about other people. Self-love means thinking about yourself first and making choices that are best for you, which most women don't do. We put others ahead every time, and then feel guilty about it! Wrong! A good guide to help improve your self-esteem is, *How to Raise Your Self-Esteem* by Nathaniel Branden.

What then do we need to achieve all these things? The following:

NEEDS LIST

Physical - We need a regular diet and exercise, which leads to a healthy body. Publications such as the *Black Women's Health Book*, *Best of Health Quarterly*, *Essence* and *Feeling Good* magazines as well as places such as Naurdi Whole Health Retreat (see Resources).

Emotional - We need to express feelings (mad, glad, sad, scared). The expression of feelings is very important.

Social - We need emotional support from our families and friends (sometimes just to get through the day!).

Intellectual - We need to satisfy our minds by informing ourselves through reading, watching television that pertains to us, and engaging in activities that enrich our drive for knowledge.

Creative - We need to express ourselves in unusual ways by trying new things that we have never considered before, while it doesn't have to be "way out," we might learn to prepare our favorite meal in a different way or try something that we have never done before altogether.

Spiritual - We need to believe in a higher power, while we might not all be card-carrying Baptists, Methodists, or Pentecostals we can believe in a power higher than ourselves, which gives us something to rely on in times of distress.

The whole concept of empowerment can truly be summed up as learning our ABC's. Learning to express ourselves, becoming more assertive in our behavior, taking control of our lives and not trying to control others. This is really all it takes. It can be, and is, that simple.

RESOURCES

The following organizations provide services specifically for us!

American Institute for Economic Development (AIED)
715 Eighth St., S.E.
Washington, D.C. 20003

American Association for Affirmative Action (AAAA)
11 E. Hubbard St., Suite 200
Chicago, IL 60611
Judith Burnison, Exec. Dir.
(312) 329-2512

Alpha Kappa Alpha Sorority
5656 S. Stony Island Ave.
Chicago, IL 60637
Nan D. Johnson, Exec. Officer
(312) 684-1281

"Best of Health"
(a quarterly newsletter for Black women)
P.O. Box 401232
Brooklyn, NY 11240-1232

Black Psychiatrists of America
c/o Dr. Thelissa Harris
664 Prospect
Hartford, CN 06105
(203) 236-2320

Coalition of Minority Women in Business
1535 P Street, N.W.
Washington, D.C. 20005

Delta Sigma Theta Sorority
1707 New Hampshire, N.W.
Washington, D.C. 20009
(202) 483-5460

Essence Magazine
1500 Broadway
New York City, NY
(212) 640-0600

Feelin' Good Magazine for Black Women
400 Corporate Pointe, Suite 580
Culver City, CA 90230
(213) 649-3320

Girl Friends
c/o Konnetta P. Sparks
237 Ardsley Road
Scarsdale, NY 10583
(914) 723-6603

Institute on Black Chemical Abuse
2616 Nicollet Avenue, S.
Minneapolis, MN 55408
612 871-7878

Lupus Foundation of America, Inc.
1717 Massachusetts Avenue, NW
Washington, D.C. 20036
(800) 558-0121

Minority Business Information Institute
130 Fifth Ave., 10th Fl.
New York, NY 10011
(212) 242-8000

National Association of Black and
Minority Chambers of Commerce
654 13th Street
Oakland, CA 94612

National Abortion Rights Action League
(NARAL)
1101 14th Street, NW
Washington, D.C. 20005
(202) 408-4600

National Association of Black Social Workers
642 Beckwith Ct., S.W.
Atlanta, GA 30314
(404) 584-7967

National Association of Black Women Lawyers
3711 Macomb St., N.W. 2nd Fl.
Washington, D.C. 20016
(202) 966-9693

National Association of Black Women Entrepreneurs
P.O. Box 1375
Detroit, MI 48231
(313) 341-7400

National Association for Sickle Cell Diseases, Inc.
3345 Wilshire Blvd., Suite 1106
Los Angeles, CA 90010-1880
213 736-5455

National Bar Association
1225 11th St., N.W.
Washington, D.C. 20001
(202) 842-3900

National Beauty Culturists' League
25 Logan Circle, N.W.
Washington, D.C. 20005
(202) 332-2695

National Black Alcoholism Council
Attn: Maxine Womble
1629 K Street, Suite 802
Washington, D.C. 20006
(202) 296-2696

National Black Child Development Institute
1463 Rhode Island Ave., N.W.
Washington, D.C. 20005
(202) 387-1281

National Black Nurses Association, Inc.
1011 North Capitol Street NE
Washington, D.C. 20002
(202) 898-5232

National Black Women's Health Project
175 Trinity Ave., S.W., 2nd Floor
Atlanta, GA 30310
(404) 681-4554

Naundi Whole Health Retreat Center
P. O. Box 9236
Allentown, PA 18105
(215) 791-4984

Non Traditional Employment for Women
243 West 20th Street
New York, NY 10011
(212) 627-6252

National Dental Association
5506 Connecticut Avenue, NW
Suite 24-25
Washington, D.C. 20015
(202) 244-7555

National Medical Association
1012 Tenth Street NW
Washington, D.C. 20001
(202) 347-1895

National Minority Aids Counsel
300 I Street NE, Suite 400
Washington, D.C. 20002
(202) 541-7800

Planned Parenthood
810 Seventh Avenue
New York, NY 10019
(212) 603-4600

National Association of Black Psychologists
P. O. Box 55999
Washington, D.C., 20040-5999
(202) 722-0808

Sisterhood of Black Single Mothers
360 Fulton St., Suite 432
Brooklyn, NY 11216
(718) 638-0413

Wider Opportunities for Women
1325 G. Street, N.W.
Washington, D.C. 20005

SELECTED BIBLIOGRAPHY

This is a partial listing of books that are listed in this book that reflect "ourstory."

Black American Information Directory
Darren Smith, Editor
Gale Research Inc.
835 Penobscot Bldg.
Detroit, MI 48226-4094

New York, Ft. Lauderdale
Black Resource Guide, Inc.
501 Oneida Place, N.W.
Washington, D.C. 20011

The Black Woman's Career Guide 2nd Ed.
Beatrice Nivens
Doubleday Anchor Press
New York City, New York
1991

The Black Woman's Health Book
Evelyn Smith (Ed)
Seal Press
Seattle, Washington
1990

The Color Purple
Alice Walker
Simon & Schuster
New York City, New York
1982

The Colored Museum
George Wolfe
Grove Press
New York City, New York
1988

The Conspiracy to Destroy Black Boys I-III
Dr. Jawanza Kunjufu
African American Images
Chicago, Illinois
1990

Developing Positive Self-Esteem in Black Children
Dr. Jawanza Kunjufu
African American Images
Chicago, Illinois
1989

Disappearing Acts
Terry McMillan
Viking Penguin
New York City, New York
1988

The Minority Executive's Handbook
Randolph Cameron
Warner Books
New York City, New York

The Black Women's Beauty Book from Inside Out:
A Guide for Black Women
LaVerne Powlis
Doubleday
New York City, New York
1991

Memory of Kin
Mary Helen Washington
Anchor Press
New York City, New York
1991

Oh, The Places You'll Go
Dr. Seuss
Random House
New York City, New York
1989

One Foot in Each World
Leanita McClain
University of Chicago Press
Chicago, Illinois
1987

The Piano Lesson
August Wilson
Plume Press
New York City, New York
1990

The Street
Ann Petry
Beacon Press
Boston, Massachusetts
1946

Tar Beach
Faith Ringold
Crown Publishers
New York City, New York
1991

A Woman's Place
Marita Golden
Ballentine Books
New York City, New York
1986

How to: Raise Your Self-Esteem
Nathanel Branden
Bantam
New York City, New York

Long Distance Life
Marita Golden
Doubleday, 1989
New York City, New York